WHAT

Live Your Legacy effectively combines the instructions of nine life changing lessons, wrapped in a heartfelt parable that is sure to inspire.

Kary Oberbrunner: Author of *Your Secret Name*, *The Deeper Path*, and *Day Job to Dream Job*

Legacy=legs! Who will walk the walk and talk the talk when you are gone? Ken challenges us to ask these questions now because legacy is something we create today. Legacy is about your journey — it's about taking others to the places they've been longing to go. Ken allows us to listen to a conversation that will change your life, transform your leadership and have you living your legacy! His life has transformed our legacy. We are so grateful.

Sarah & Phil Robbins:
Network Marketing professionals

Ken has written a book that will inspire all who read it to reach their highest potential and live by design rather than default.

Tommy Barnett: Author, Co-pastor of Dream City Church, in Phoenix, Arizona, Founder of the L.A. International Dream Center and chancellor of Southeastern University

Live Your Legacy is an amazing gift that will give you a road map to live an impactful life. This book gave me a love punch and will cause lasting change in the direction of my life. Thank you Ken for the wake-up call.

Jeff Latham: President and Founder at Latham Realty Unlimited

Outstanding! Ken's easy-to-read writing style is loaded with life lessons that everyone needs to know. This book is full of profound insights that once applied will make our lives valuable for generations to come.

Craig Wendel: Lead pastor at SouthPoint Church in Southaven, Mississippi

What an incredible book that moves its readers from struggle to freedom and the steps it took to get there. This is one of those rare life changing reads that everyone needs to experience.

Jake Sellers: Co-founder of Jesus Unified Inc., an organization dedicated to rescuing women and children from sex trafficking

Live Your Legacy is a powerful story that causes you to reflect deeply on your own life. Ken is a master of finding transformational messages and packaging them in a way that elevates people's lives. In this book, he leads you on a journey that inspires you to take action on nine life lessons that will change your life if you act on them.

Coyte Cooper: Ph.D., Bestselling Author, Keynote Speaker, Coach, TEDx Speaker

Live Your Legacy is a powerful resource of truth in action. Ken does an incredible job of moving us from inspiration into practical application. You will be blessed by his transparency, wisdom, and personal story of God's redeeming power.

Katie Farrell: Author of *Dashing Dish, and Devotions for a Healthier You*

LIVE YOUR LEGACY

9 LIFE LESSONS TO LIVING A LIFE WORTH PASSING ON

KEN HUBBARD

Printed in the United States of America. Published by
Author Academy Elite P.O. Box 43, Powell, OH 43035.
www.AuthorAcademyElite.com.

Cover designed by Fairy@99

Ken Hubbard
Visit my website at www.KenHubbard.org

Paperback ISBN-978-1-64085-471-0
Hardcover ISBN-978-1-64085-472-7
E-book ISBN-978-1-64085-473-4

Library of Congress Control Number: 2018960013

Dedication

To my wife Patti.

You have been my inspiration for over 30 years now. You have helped me live a legacy that at one time I thought was only for other people. I can't even begin to imagine my journey without you. I love you so much.

To my son, Jake, and his wife, Carmen, and my beautiful daughter, Jenessa. I am so proud of you all. Keep living the nine.

Table of Contents

Part 3: The Reveal

"Legacy is not what we leave behind for others to receive, rather it's what we deposit in people for them to achieve"

Ken Hubbard

Preface

I never could imagine how a cup a coffee with an old man could so radically change the direction of my life, but it did. To say this chance encounter impacted my life in such a way that even my kids are reaping the benefits is an understatement.

The old man is not a counselor or a coach. Just alone, accompanied only by the haunting memories of mistakes made and the wishful thinking of doing things differently.

I encourage you to pour yourself a cup of coffee, pull up a chair, and listen to the conversation between an old man disappointed with the legacy he will leave behind, and a young man searching for answers to the questions left behind by the accidents and incidents of life. He now has an opportunity to redeem some regrets and build a living legacy on the nine nuggets of truth revealed in the pages that follow.

If hurt and disappointment give us insight, then this old man has it. Perhaps in life there are two teachers: revelation or situation.

The old man was taught by life's tough and painful situations. Maybe the young man can learn through revelation. If you're looking for conventional, he is not it. He is not even that happy of an old man, at least not yet.

Legacy = anything handed down from the past, as from an ancestor or predecessor.

We often think of legacy as something we leave behind. What if we begin to live a life with the legacy in mind? Maybe instead of leaving a legacy, we should consider living a legacy. Come hang out with me and this old man and find out how.

PART ONE
The Regrets

"A man is not old until regrets take the place of his dreams."

John Barrymore

1

Coffee in a Fog

I held the coffee cup with both hands as I warmed myself beside the fireplace. That first drink of my tall white chocolate Americano felt and tasted so good going down on this cold, rainy day. A typical April day in the Pacific Northwest, Ristretto Coffee Shop lay somewhere between here and there. Tucked away in a quaint little town that looked like time had forgotten, but the steady flow of customers would suggest otherwise. Somehow, I felt safe there. Maybe it was the surrounding mountains or the obscurity of it all, but I felt safe. I found comfort in the fact that I couldn't possibly be identified by anyone, which allowed me to sink into my thoughts and further consider my journey, left alone to wrestle with the questions that I had come to ponder.

The old brass bell that rang when the door was opened sounded a bit like a bell choir in what otherwise seemed like a quiet town. That bell again interrupting my thoughts as customers added to those already waiting in line. Diverse customers it seemed for such a small town. Young and old, white collar and blue. Some in groups talking and strategizing their day. Some quiet and alone. Everyone assembled there like runners at a starting line, waiting for today's race to begin.

I sat there in this worn, overstuffed leather chair in a town I didn't recognize, surrounded by people I didn't know, and I didn't care to. I was invisible and comfortable and content in my cocoon of self-reflection.

Because focusing on me and my objective was too painful, I began to focus on those in the room. Some observation and a little eavesdropping had me judging and critiquing. In my mind I was even attempting to give them advice. I pretended to know them and their plot as they assembled in line. The guy in the suit I imagined to be a lawyer preparing for a big case. The guy next to him, a car salesman, who at that moment was too busy on his phone to give any greeting to the barista trying to understand his order. Next, a construction worker, dressed in his Carhartt overalls complete with work boots. A teacher, a student, a nurse, and the policeman were all easy to identify.

Each person on their own journey, huddled for a moment in time, then off in multiple directions, like a crack on a windshield splintering and progressing in multiple directions while pursuing their agendas and goals for the day. Each facing challenges and perhaps fears, trying their best to solve the questions that face us all in life. Why does the guy in the flannel shirt refuse to look up or make eye contact with anyone? How about the loud, overconfident guy, greeting everyone, his voice beckoning over the crowd? Was he over compensating for some hidden insecurities? There in the corner, the girl with the earphones, and eyes glued to her tablet. Was she alone, did she have friends?

It became a game to evaluate and speculate about each person who came in and rang the brass bell. I tried to read their body language, observing the way they placed their order, even the tone in their voices. I found it much easier to speculate about their lives than to evaluate mine.

Reality check. That's why I am here drinking coffee in a heavy fog. A fog so thick you can't seem to see but a couple steps in front of where you're going. I am here to evaluate, I guess, maybe discover, even try to understand the little boy that I see in the mirror every day. That little boy in the mirror is now wearing a man's body, fully grown on the outside but not so much on the inside, and is still trying to heal, understand, make sense out of who I am supposed to be.

It has been 20 years since I had been in this wet wonderland of evergreen and cedar. Populated by majestic mountains and foggy beaches, I was back. I wasn't here seeking its beauty, but seeking answers, or maybe just trying to discover and better understand the questions. The questions I have spent my life wrestling with, they seem to weigh me down and limit my vision like this heavy fog cover on this gloomy morning. I am not even sure what questions I want answered or what ones to ask, though I have rehearsed them many times in the last twenty years. Questions about my purpose, identity, about marriage, parenting, career, and wondering if he thought about me as often as I thought about him. I feel like I have a giant question mark on my chest, and I desperately want to exchange it for a Big Red "S". I know that's taking it a little too far, I would even be satisfied with a small "s". That would be sufficient.

If Clark Kent could never understand who he was, his identity, his purpose, his strengths, and even his weaknesses, he would have continued to write stories, instead of creating stories and becoming Superman.

It's not Superman I want to become, just a healthy man, able to leap over the obstacles of insecurities that often keep me grounded. How do I overcome the feelings of shame and rejection that plague me like Superman's kryptonite all while exhausting myself trying to look strong and confident?

Is the answer somewhere between here and there drinking coffee? Somewhere between where I am and where I desperately want to be, I wonder if I can find him. And if I do, will he have some answers for me? Or will this encounter only fuel the anger and hurt that constantly plagues me? It's been twenty years since I have seen him or heard from him. How will I feel when I see him? Will he reject me? Will we shake hands or hug? I feel so awkward just thinking about it. Apprehensive to say the least, but I have concluded it's worth the risk. At least I did until I got here. It's better than not knowing, I think. If I find him, I might find myself or at least some clues to help me discover me.

Do I call him Dad? Father sounds too formal. Pops sounds like an old man. I haven't used the word Dad in so many years it is like a foreign language is coming out of my mouth. I was five when he came into my room and informed me he had to leave. He wasn't sure when he would see me next. It was late, and I was in bed, so I wasn't even sure what that meant. I have vivid memories of him, partly because they are few and partly because I have played them over in my mind so many times. I see them like it was yesterday.

Occasionally, I get a smell of dirt that takes me back like a time machine, to the back yard, as we dug roads in the dirt for my Tonka trucks. Like a sculptor, he carved and dug as I waited patiently making truck noises. He removed rocks and cut roots, so the trucks could pass without complication through the make-believe gravel pit in my backyard. It's like a movie in my mind, played over and over. One of the removed rocks created such a hole that he had to build a bridge with scrap metal that he repurposed from the garage. That bridge became my favorite place to pass in the journey of those make-believe guys trying to deliver their cargo in the world of my back yard. Maybe I am just holding on to hope that he still holds some ability to magically help me dig up some rocks, bridge some gaps, and cut some roots...a bridge to help me understand the why's of life.

Why do I act certain ways? Why do I feel so alone in the midst of a crowd? Why do I lose my temper so easily? Why do I possess the unquenchable need to make people like me? Why do I like the mayonnaise on the bread and not between the meat and cheese?

The answers are more than a passing curiosity. I want desperately for my tomorrows to be better than my yesterdays, but all I see is a gap and I desperately need a bridge. I got married a couple years

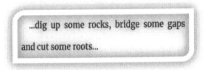

...dig up some rocks, bridge some gaps and cut some roots...

ago, now we are talking kids!? I am excited and afraid all at the same time. Do I have what it takes? Do I have the emotional and spiritual stamina to run the race set before me? I don't want to spend my life punching a time clock without a purpose. When I am alone, and no-one is looking, I still cry the way I did when we separated. Do I have the strength to lift the rocks, or the skill to build the bridges. There seems to be a hole, a gap if you will, between where I am at and where or who I desperately want to be. I am stuck somewhere between here and there in a fog.

I know the answers aren't here drinking coffee. Unless he is here! What if he was? Would I recognize him? The longer I sit, the more I second guess this trip. Is it possible that living with the questions is better than getting the answers I might not like? Maybe I don't want to know after all. That familiar feeling of anxiety is beginning to creep in again. I know I am stalling, procrastinating again for sure. Arguing with myself, lost in my self-absorbed thoughts, my mind is racing again as it often does, thankfully rescued by the sound of that old brass bell, bringing me back to the coffee shop.

The interruption caused me to look up and lay eyes on an old man. It wasn't hard to conclude that he didn't blend in with the younger and somewhat trendy company that occupied the coffee shop. He shuffled to the counter to place his order. Another stranger, another story, I surmised.

"Black. I'll take mine black, none of that sweet fu-fu candy stuff," I heard him grumble to the barista. His face was weathered and wrinkled as though he had lived a hard life, but his eyes seemed to be filled with as much or more regret than mine. I guess it takes one to know one. Yes, it's his eyes. They look...

Familiar? Maybe. Impossible! Probably just my melancholy mood, but they did seem to tell a story all on their own. Kind of deliberate. Squinting his eyes as though they were searching for something or someone. As much as I wanted to remain in my cocoon ignored by everyone, there was something about him that made me curious. What's behind those wrinkles? What triumphs and tragedies were behind the years he had lived. Not today, I thought, I have my own agenda, I was birthing my own wrinkles. I watched him take his first sip of hot, black coffee and begin to search the room for a place to sit. Then I noticed that this busy coffee shop only offered one single chair. Yep, the matching overstuffed leather chair next to me at the fireplace. Old leather, how appropriate. I quickly looked away and put on my best "deep in thought, don't bother me" look. I had better things to do than to be held hostage by an old grouchy man with nothing better to do than to reminisce with someone who hadn't heard all his stories.

My selfish thoughts and my unfriendly look were interrupted by a gravelly voice, in a grumpy tone asking, "Is this chair taken?"

"No sir," I responded, trying not to make eye contact.

"Great! I could use a warm fire and a young man's conversation."

2

Conversation with a Stranger

onversation!? That is the last thing that I want. Topics quickly rushed through my mind of conversation I might be subjected to: the weather, his aches and pains, or what kind of medicine he is taking. I thought about getting up and leaving, but then I would have to stop procrastinating and get on with my journey. Maybe a conversation with a stranger is just the diversion I need to escape the realities of why I am here.

He slowly lowered himself into the newer of the two leather chairs next to me sighing loud and long as he sank into it, as though he was releasing the burden of a long hard journey. I tried hard to put off a "don't bother me, I am not friendly" vibe. Given his tough exterior, that tactic wouldn't work with him. Clearly, intimidation had long left his company.

"You're not from around these parts, are you?" he asked in a somewhat demanding tone.

I dared not ignore him or even try to brush him off. Something about him demanded my attention.

"No," I replied.

"Not many outsiders here in this valley unless they are lost," he spouted.

If he only knew. That's exactly what I am! I thought. Lost, not physically, but, emotionally and internally, I was lost.

There was a long pause, I sensed he was waiting for me to dive into where I was from and why I was there. The silence was awkward. I glanced up to give him a courtesy smile, if for no other reason than to ease my conscience. Making eye contact for a moment is all it took to arrest my attention. His eyes seemed to tell a story. He seemed to be waiting for the right moment to share some of life's wisdom and experiences. And with one glance, I was out of my cocoon.

"I guess you could say I am on a journey," I began as I took another sip of my coffee. "I was born not far from here. I have come back after 20 years or so just to….um, well…" Not really knowing what to say, the words 'connect the dots' came out of my mouth.

"That can be a good thing. The more dots you connect, the clearer the picture becomes," the old man said with a bit of a smirk.

It was with that statement I realized that a conversation with a stranger was just what I needed. He doesn't have anything to gain or lose. It's not like he knows anyone I know. I will never see him again. This could be free entertainment or therapy. It seemed so impersonal and disrespectful, but I was thinking that he didn't have many years left on this earth anyway. The intrigue of this old guy was begging me to ask questions, questions that might release years of wisdom and insights, kind of like the whole connecting the dots thing.

The more dots you connect, the clearer the picture becomes.

He cleared his throat and began to expound on his thoughts. The tone of his voice elevated my interest. Non-sympathetic, mixed with a little pain and hardness had me picturing him as an old fishing boat captain.

"It's a sad thing that more people don't take the time to connect some dots. It draws the picture. It draws the target. Without the picture or target, we will never get to where we are going."

Exactly! I thought.

He continued, "I 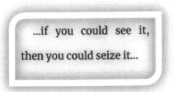 always believed that if you could see something, then you could seize it. Life is made up of many travels and adventures. From dot to dot we go. Some dots you arrive at, some are sad, some happy, triumphant and tragic, good dots and bad dots. The key is to never get stuck on a bad dot. There are also dots that just mark another year gone by."

"How many dots have you had," I asked with a smile knowing it was way too early in the conversation to get so personal, but I wanted to get an idea of how old he was.

"I quit counting those dots a long time ago," he responded with a none of your business kind of tone.

"You see, it's what lies between the dots that really matter. We can't always avoid the bad dots in life as we draw the lines. It's more about how we navigate in between the good and the bad dots. Yep, that's what paints our life picture. You must live a while before you recognize what your picture looks like. It's not the dots, but how you handle them and how you move from each one. I often wished that connecting dots came with an eraser," he said as he gazed into the fire as though something from the past still haunted him with regret.

"Do you like your picture," I asked.

"Well, it's not finished. Don't put me in the grave yet! I am still working on it," as he turned his gaze away from the fire and back to me.

"The truth is that there are many lines I would like to eliminate and others I retrace in my mind as often as I can. Usually on Mondays."

"Mondays?"

"Mondays. I leave the house and tell regret to stay home. I order a black coffee and sit in that chair," he said, pointing at the older looking of the two chairs, which happened to be the one I was sitting in. "I sit there and retrace the good in-betweens. I've worn them as thin as that old chair over the years. Memory tries to escape me from time to time. The color fades off occasionally leaving me with the vague gray versions of a once vibrant colorful memory. I would be lost without them. So, I come here to retrace, trying to make sure they don't get forgotten. I sure wished there were more," he said with as much weight as I was feeling just a bit earlier.

"This chair?" I questioned, trying to lighten the mood.

"Yep. That's how I knew you weren't from around here."

"Please sit here! I'll trade with you," I insisted.

"Oh no. Feels good to sit in a different seat. Kind of gives a fresh perspective. Makes me feel younger, less worn out," he said with a twinkle in his eye. "Probably won't be long before they throw that old chair out anyway. Besides, this is the day for you to connect some dots. Sit back and enjoy its comfort as you draw your masterpiece."

He spoke like he knew something, or at least like he wanted to say something. I first chalked it up to an old man wanting someone to talk to. But he made me feel like he knew what I was going through, like he had been there himself in days gone by. The more we talked the more comfortable I was in his presence. I sat back and relaxed as he began to reflect. I could feel my self-defense begin to subside as my curiosity began to increase. I wanted to know him, I wanted to know about his "dots" and "lines". He began to ramble about life challenges. I wondered if maybe he was trying to justify or even feel better about mistakes and difficulties that he had encountered along his journey.

"What would you erase, if you had an eraser?" I questioned.

"Getting kind of personal, aren't you?" I couldn't tell if he was snarling at me or the regrets. "I told you

I make regrets wait at home on Mondays. They try hard to follow. Most days they succeed," he admitted.

"Maybe you could use them to help a guy that's just trying to connect the right dots," I sheepishly stated.

There was an awkward silence again. Had I stepped on a nerve? He stared at his empty coffee cup. I was waiting for his response as though I was waiting for some great prize. It was surreal, the metamorphosis that had taken place between us in such a short time. Just a few moments ago I didn't want him to talk to me, now I am hoping he will. Staring into his cup as though it was filled with a lifetime of memories, trying to fish out the things he might share, even wondering if he would or if he should. Suddenly, well not so suddenly, he stood up. Was this where the conversation ended?

When he reached his upright position, he looked down at me and said, "Eighty-three. Eighty-three dots. Pretty sure my picture is complete I don't do too much dot connecting anymore, but maybe today I will add a little color to my old black and white life. But first I am gonna get another cup of coffee."

As I waited for him to return with his coffee, I realized I was like a kid eager to have grandpa tell of his childhood stories. I sat watching him, wondering how the conversation would unfold, and who would be the beneficiary? Could it be that I was helping him as he is helping me? A little over dramatic, maybe so. I guess time will tell.

PART TWO
The Reverse

"You can't go back and make a new start, but you can start right now and make a brand-new ending"

James R. Sherman

3

Take Out The Trash

My thoughts are interrupted when I notice that as he was waiting for his second cup of coffee, he seems a bit irritated, even disgusted, looking into the overflowing trash can. The busy morning has left them overflowing. I watch with suspicion as he begins to bundle up the garbage, as though he was an employee, then making eye contact with me to get up and come over to him. I am a bit puzzled as I walk toward him. He hands me the garbage bag and tells me there is a green dumpster out back, followed by complete details of what door to use and what directions to follow.

Wait! One minute ago, I am lost in my thoughts minding my own business. Now I am out in the rain and fog taking out trash as ordered by an old man that

I didn't want to talk to in the first place! Now I am doing chores for him? In a coffee shop?

Chilled from the outside air, I reentered the coffee shop to find him warmly seated in the old leather chair, by the fire, taking a sip from his second cup of coffee. I am sure there is still a perplexed look on my face. He speaks before I can gather my thoughts and say anything.

"Always take out the trash!" he exclaimed.

Okay, I am thinking in a sarcastic tone.

"That's what my wife, God rest her soul, used to remind me of all the time. Ex-wife that is. Our marriage ended close to five years into it. Never had any kids. Sometimes I wished we did, but most of the time I am glad we didn't put any innocent kids through the pain. I sure loved her."

For the first time I heard a crack in his old hardened voice, as what appeared to be a tear form in the corner of his eye to run down his weathered cheek. He quickly wiped it away, hoping I didn't notice it.

"That's why I wish for an eraser," he said. "I would erase the divorce that has plagued me with regret from the day it was final. I didn't stay alone the rest of my life, but I sure have stayed lonely."

I quietly listened and wondered if he somehow knew I was wrestling with my own marriage challenges, feelings of inadequacy, and not being good enough. "If you don't mind me asking, why did you divorce?" I couldn't believe I was so forward, but the intensity of his regret could be felt, and curiosity was begging to know. "Did she do you wrong? Did she not love you? What happened?" I asked.

"She loved me way more than I deserved," he quickly defended. "She never did me wrong, she treated me with grace, she believed in me, she did everything to make it work. I loved her, too, and wanted to spend the rest of my life with her. There isn't a day that goes by I don't regret losing her. Even on Mondays, when I am trying to retrace the vivid color of the day we met. It was a Monday. One of the good dots. My mind often likes to imagine an alternate story line, but always ends with bitter reality, then regret."

"Well, what happened?" I asked, trying to not look too eager, realizing I was on the edge of my newer leather chair.

He cleared his throat as though he was trying to erase the pain and spoke in the softest voice I had heard come out of him. "I guess you could say I refused to take out the trash."

"Wait! What? You mean to tell me you both loved each other, she treated you great, but you didn't take out the trash and poof she is gone?"

"You got a lot to learn," he replied. "I am not talking about the trash under the sink, not the trash the garbage man takes away every Tuesday. I am talking about the trash that accumulates in our soul, that clutters our thinking and contaminates our hopes.

"Imagine this coffee shop for a moment," he said. "It's a nice warm place with the great smell of coffee brewing, friends conversing, and old men reminiscing. All that can be ruined by the smell and view of an overflowing trash can."

"I think I get it," I said.

"When we married," he continued, "I brought baggage to our home, full of trash. Hurts from words spoken at me in anger for much of my childhood, unforgiveness for wrongs done. Accidents, and incidents. Most people have them. I guess we all have garbage, but you gotta take it out and leave it out. Otherwise, it will stink up your life," he continued.

"I was grumpy."

That's not a surprise, I reminded myself.

"More than grumpy, I was defensive and mad. Any disagreement ended with my anger, nothing resolved. Just the woman I loved, shutting down, slowly but surely building walls to protect. Hurt by the man she loved. I was never angry at her, I just had unresolved hurt in my own life and it came out in anger toward anybody that I wrongly thought was a threat because I was never going to be hurt again. I guess when you hurt inside, you hurt others without even trying to. Yep, I let the trash of unforgiveness and unresolved hurts overflow into our home and it made quite a stink. Unforgiveness made me feel empowered. It made me feel like I was punishing those people and circumstances that had once hurt me and betrayed me. The truth is, it was slowly killing me and anyone that tried to be close to me. The walls I built to protect myself only closed her out. She remarried, had kids and showered them with love. Love that I could have had. She died about six years ago. I reluctantly attended the funeral. I quietly slipped in late, so not to be noticed and listened from the back row. Two kids and six grandkids

> ...when you hurt inside, you often hurt others...

and one great grandchild. Friends and family spoke of her life. They talked about how she loved her family and poured it into her kids and grandkids. They mentioned her adventurous spirit, her sweet disposition. Pictures of family vacations, graduations, birthdays, and Christmases. It seemed they mentioned everything I remembered loving about her. One thing they didn't mention though."

"Really? What?" I needed to know.

"Me," he replied with a sigh. "They never mentioned me. I slipped out before anyone would ask who I was or how I was connected to her. As I drove home I realized that the life she lived and the legacy she left behind could have been mine, if I would have only taken out the trash. I wasted a lot of years holding onto hurt."

"I don't know what hurts life has thrown your way," he said to me, "But don't ever let someone's dysfunction of the past hold you hostage of your today and destroy your tomorrow."

I felt a lump in my throat as I listened with great respect. I knew this was a defining moment and I had some trash to take out before I continued my journey.

"That's all I feel like talking about today," he stated. As he stood to leave, I wondered if this would be the last time I would see or hear from him.

Not wanting our time to end, I said, "I don't even know your name."

"Not important," he said.

Desperately not wanting to lose his company or end our conversation I managed to ask, "Coffee tomorrow?"

"Maybe," he replied.

"Well, I will be here at the same time tomorrow and coffee is on me, black, none of that fu-fu candy stuff," I managed to say.

Halfway to the door he turned and said, "You can't connect dots without something to write with. If I am gonna take the time to share, you should write it down. After all, you can't hit a target if you don't draw the bullseye."

Without having a chance to respond, he turned again, slipped out into the fog and disappeared. I realized he had just delivered a second nugget of truth. *You can't hit the target that you don't see.* I was also lost in the thought of how familiar his past was to mine. Somehow, I needed to take note and adhere to the wisdom of this old sage. I got up out of my chair and for the second time today, took out the trash.

4

The Tattered Page

It was too early to return to my hotel room, not to mention my newfound energy I needed to burn off. A walk through this little town might help me process the wisdom that had just been downloaded to me. It wasn't just the wisdom, that had me mesmerized - it was the whole encounter. I was still trying to wrap my mind around it all. Why was I so open to conversation with this old man? Furthermore, I was already hoping he would show up in the morning.

The sidewalks were much more alive than they were earlier in the morning. As I looked through the jumble of people, I noticed the name of a used bookstore, "The Tattered Page." As I approached the store window, it occurred to me that purchasing a pen and a notepad might be wise. I wanted to record my newly found insights and be prepared for the possibility of my morning's class. I had once heard it said that the shortest pencil is better than the longest memory, and I didn't want to forget what I had learned, or what I might hear.

I expected a little brass bell to announce my arrival, but silence greeted me as I entered the store. The smell of old musty books filled the air and the shelves were stacked to overflowing - even stacks on the floor and on tables. Each book has its own life. Though the authors are probably dead and gone, their stories live on forever in those pages just waiting in this warehouse of books to be opened and released. Stories of truth and fiction, adventures and biographies, how to, and what ifs. Because of the mood I was in, I found myself suddenly consumed with the urge to submerge myself into every story.

My thoughts were interrupted by a polite lady with the typical librarian bun in her hair, "Can I help you?"

"I am in need of pen and paper," I announced.

"Unless it's used, we don't have it here," she answered. "I do have a couple old journals," she continued as she quickly disappeared before I could respond.

Great. What would I do with someone's used journal I thought. She returned with two journals and began to describe each one with more enthusiasm than anyone should have over an old journal.

"This one is a hard cover and it looks like someone recorded their favorite fishing holes and stories in it, probably filled with stories of 'the one that got away,'" she said obviously trying to be funny.

"This one might be something you could use," she said, as she held up an old soft leather journal with a flap on it that immediately had me thinking of the old man as it looked like it was made from the same leather as the old chairs we sat in.

"Only one page has been written on," she noted, as she fanned the pages stopping on page one and reading the words penned at the top of the first page by an unknown writer.

My Journey. That was it? That's all they wrote? I couldn't help but wonder what happened. Why was there only two words? Had the journal been lost? Did their journey end too soon? Or did it even get started? Did the journey end abruptly?

My recent conversation had me emboldened with feelings of new resolve and determination not to allow my journey to be compromised or interrupted. I determined that I would fill in the pages of a journey well-traveled, a life well lived.

"I'll take it," I proclaimed with enthusiasm, as I dished out a whopping $3.99 plus tax.

Upon returning to my hotel room with my newly found treasure, I opened it to record the words I had received earlier in the day under the heading *My Journey* I wrote **#1 *Take out the Trash.***

Those two statements on the same page seemed to work in partnership causing me to have further revelation. If my journey is going to go any farther, I must lighten the load and take out some trash. I was unaware and unprepared for the flood of emotions that the partnership of words would release. Suddenly, words with intense emotion began to flow like a dam had just burst.

It wasn't hard to write. In fact, it's as though I couldn't write fast enough. Memories that had been ignored and left to live deep in the basement of my mind for many years began to surface as my pen

> If my journey is going to go any farther, I must lighten the load.

raced across the page trying to keep up with the trash that had been overlooked for too many years, begging to be released from the prison of my mind. Putting them on paper seemed to release them from my soul giving them a place to live and no longer holding me hostage. I never imagined that I had so much to write about. As I recorded the long-buried memories that hadn't seen the light of day in many years, the accidents, words, embarrassments, and rejections, I could feel them leave me.

It was almost magical. The more pain I expelled to the journal, the more peace I felt in my soul. At times my pen paused to confront the memory, even yell at the person or circumstance that had created the imprint as though they were in the room with me. Other times my pen needed to stop and release the pain and sadness from a memory that had been ignored and was now asking for just a bit of acknowledgment. As the day rolled into night, the breakthrough was obvious. I was exhausted and triumphant at the same time. I looked in the mirror above the desk I was sitting at realizing that that little boy I saw in the mirror just grew up a little today. I dropped my pen and closed my journal and smiled at myself in the mirror as I realized that I had just taken out the trash for the third time today.

Before I turned off the lights, in honor of all I had written, I labeled the following blank page:

#2 *Write it down*.

It was in writing in that journal that I realized the power in writing down my breakthroughs. I laughed as I further realized the old man had taught me another lesson without even trying. Or was he trying?

Documenting what I learned would be a way I could be reminded of the lesson after the emotion of the moment had worn off. It also would become a transcript that I could share with my wife or others without forgetting the details. Maybe I should not only write down the lessons learned, but the adventures I had or desired to have. And what about dreams and values? If I want to hit the target, then I have to draw the bullseye. This journal would become the bullseye, my tool for change. After all, didn't he say *if I could see it, I could seize it*? He might be a little grumbly, but that old guy is pretty clever. I will be prepared for tomorrow with my new journal and a pen in hand. Tomorrow, I choose to seize it!

5

Walk Tall

I slept well that night, although I woke to look at the clock a few times, with anticipation of morning, hoping and wondering if he would be there. I was eager to get up and get my journey underway. I must admit that I was enjoying the diversion from wrestling with the anxiety that came with the uncertainty of finding my dad.

The sun finally made its morning appearance and began the process of burning off the thin marine layer that wove softly through the valley. Needing to burn up some nervous energy, I grabbed my newly found treasure from the Tattered Page and walked the few blocks to the coffee house. I wanted to be early enough to get our seats by the fire. My mind began to form questions I wanted to ask. I wondered what conversations we might have, what nuggets I could learn, and why did I feel so compelled to hear what he had to say?

As I opened the door, the little bell of the coffee shop rang again to announce me as the day's first customer.

"I'll take a white chocolate Americano, and I'll pay for a black coffee - for the old man."

"Will he be here today?" questioned the young lady behind the counter.

"I am not sure, but I am hoping so," I replied.

"I am guessing he must have family in from out of town. Are you his grandson?" she asked

"No, I just met him yesterday. Why do you think he has family in town?" I questioned.

"Well, last Monday I saw him have a brief conversation with a man standing at the window. Then yesterday, the two of you hung out and talked as if you knew each other quite well. I have served him black coffee every Monday for a while now and he sits over there in that old leather chair that you were sitting in. Everyone around here knows on Monday that's the old man's chair. We have wanted to throw it out, but were afraid to on account of him. He doesn't engage in much conversation, just the occasional greeting, and barking out his coffee order. By the way, what's his name?" she asked with a 'tell me a secret' kind of tone.

"I don't know," I replied. "I actually just met him yesterday. If the truth be told I was trying to avoid him myself. Imagine that, two guys trying to avoid conversation spent most the morning here talking."

"So, he never comes in, except for Mondays?" I inquired with a bit of disappointment.

"Only Mondays as long as I have been here," she said.

With that I paid for our drinks, thanked her and made my way to the better of the two leather chairs. From there I could see the sidewalk as I watched for his old bent over shuffled walk to appear. The little bell began to increase in its frequency as the light began to invade the outside valley, not as foggy today, things seemed a little bit clearer. One by one the regulars made their way in and out with coffee in hand to start their day.

He should have been here by now, I thought. He was here by this time yesterday. As each minute passed, I could feel my anticipation subside while my anxiety increased. I watched as the morning crowd began to subside as one by one they exited the door on their way to their day's adventures and challenges. I realized that my cup was now empty. At the same time I noticed the trash was full. I laughed to myself as I debated if I should empty it or not. I haven't learned anything if I don't put into action the things I have heard. With that, I got up to take out the trash.

"I can get that," said the girl that I had talked to earlier.

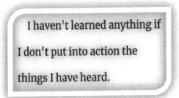

I haven't learned anything if I don't put into action the things I have heard.

"I don't mind. I'm just hanging out," I replied.

"Do you want a refund on that pre-paid coffee?" she asked, maybe trying to make me feel better about the old man not arriving.

"No," I replied. "Just pay for him next Monday," I said as I made my exit with the trash in hand. I could feel the familiar feelings of frustration and disappointment rising up as I threw the trash in the big green dumpster with much more force than necessary.

While noticing the spike in my emotions, I re-entered the back door and she greeted me, shifting her eyes and bending her head toward the chairs. There he was drinking his hot cup of black coffee.

"Good morning, and thanks for the coffee," he called across the room. Suddenly, my day got a little brighter. I walked toward him and as I was about to sit he said, "Walk taller."

"Excuse me?" I asked.

"Walk taller. That's what I would do better in between the dots. I would walk taller."

"What does that mean?" I questioned.

"I've spent so many years burdened by regret and shame that my old body won't straighten up anymore. I should have walked taller with my head up and eyes straight forward. When you have nothing left to prove and nothing left to hide you can walk tall."

And just like that, he began to share as I reached for my journal and wrote the words...

#3 Walk Tall

He talked faster than I could write as though he had thought about this for years, just waiting for the right person to listen. Come to think of it, I bet he has thought of it for years. I couldn't help but wonder why I was the guy he decided to share it with.

He talked of a childhood that was less than ideal. He didn't go into details. I suspected it was not to expose those that lived in his memory, or not wanting to dig up pain that seemed as though he had spent a lifetime burying.

"Have you ever dropped something and it broke?" he asked me?

"Oh, yeah. I dropped my grandma's ceramic yard elf. I tried gluing it back together, but it was never going to pass her eye for detail. It didn't even quite resemble an elf when I was done."

He laughed. "I know the feeling! As a child I felt like that yard elf. Dropped, and I am not sure if I ever was restored to my original beauty," he said half laughing. "I know I never walked as tall or straight as I should have," he said in a much more serious tone.

I listened intently, knowing I was hearing stories that had never left the security of his memory, like a treasure locked up and buried where no one would ever find them. I felt as though he was giving me the treasure map, and it was up to me to dig up the wealth of wisdom buried in his words.

"I have lived a life of shame," he said as though he was coming to that discovery as he was talking. "I am not sure if I had a lot a value. I think I was mostly in the way. I've concluded that those are some pretty foundational building blocks," he said.

"That's probably why I am here. I live with this overwhelming desire to know if I am valuable," I agreed.

He nodded his head in agreement. "Don't let shame take root in your life," he said. "Shame overshadows our purpose, and without purpose we live reckless and aimless, only fueling the vicious cycle of shame."

"Guilt is a little easier to deal with. When we do something wrong, we can correct the wrong and fix the guilt. But shame. Oh, shame is a whole other monster. When I am guilty, it's because I did something wrong. You can fix the wrong and make guilt evac-uate. Not so with shame. Shame tells you that you are the something wrong. I have lived most all my life with shame as my constant companion. I worked hard and ran fast to get away from shame, but I could never work hard enough or run fast enough to avoid her company."

...without purpose we live reckless and aimless...

"You know what I have learned about shame?" he asked.

"What's that?" I replied.

"Shame loves to replay those negative voices of the past. She raised her head every time I failed. She only grew stronger when I remained silent or found someone else to blame for my behavior."

I felt like he was reading my mail. "I couldn't agree more," I said. "I understand where shame comes from and what feeds her, but how do I evict her?"

"Take out the trash and while you're doing it, walk tall," he advised.

"Hmm. Can you get any more specific?" I asked.

He reached in his pocket and pulled out a twenty-dollar bill. "Would you like to have this twenty-dollar bill?" he asked with a straight face.

"Well, I wouldn't deny it," I said.

"Before you answer, imagine with me what things this twenty-dollar bill may have been used to accomplish. Maybe it was used to buy groceries for a hungry family. Yet, maybe it's had a more colorful past than that. Maybe as it made its way through life, it fell into hands that spent it to buy crack or other harmful drugs, which might have led to the destruction of a marriage, and a lonely little leaguer wondering where dad is. Maybe a father who used this twenty-dollar bill to buy a bottle of whisky, got drunk and beat his kids. Imagine all the people that have used this bill to hurt people and ruin lives."

He continued, "Think about it. This bill is pretty disgusting, if you think about all of the heartache and hurt, even the shame this bill could have caused." He was speaking as though he was the twenty-dollar bill.

"Why would you ever want this bill after hearing the history like that? Why would you ever want to drink coffee with a guy like me?" he asked.

Before I could answer, he continued giving me insight to his late arrival.

"I wasn't going to show today," he said. "Shame almost won again, but I thought that maybe my life could add some value to yours."

He crumbled the $20 bill in his hand and asked, "Do you still want this twenty-dollar bill?"

"Of course, I would! It still has value regardless of where it's been, or what it has done," I declared.

"Right!" he exclaimed. "The value isn't determined by what it's been used for or what it has been through. That's why I am back here on a Tuesday. I was created with value, and so are you," he said with conviction.

"I guess I should have learned that lesson earlier," he continued.

"What lesson?" I asked, trying to make sure I wasn't missing something.

"That a neglected childhood, the hurts and rejection, or harsh words spoken at you, don't change your value," he said as he looked me straight in the eye. "If I can help you through my mistakes, then maybe we both become more valuable. Though like this bill, I will have many more wrinkles," he said, again trying to lighten things up.

"Life will try to steal your value. People will try to devalue you also, because if they can devalue you, then it makes them feel more valuable. Walk tall. Don't let shame steal your value," he said.

"Maybe someone was supposed to love you, but they weren't there for you. Maybe words of those who were supposed to build you up, only tore you down. Now you sit here in a coffee shop wrestling with the feelings of worthlessness and procrastinating because of insecurities."

He was leaning closer and closer and I knew he was wanting me to hear. Looking me straight in the eye he said, "Walk tall. You are worth it."

Those words triggered yet another emotion in me, but a good one! I could feel tears wanting permission to run, but I held them back as best as possible. Internally, something happened. I found myself repeating... *I am worth it*!

I felt the urge to disagree, but I knew he was right.

"No matter what mistakes you've made or pain you've endured, your value is not determined by what you've done or been through," he continued. "I am old now and I have nothing left to prove and nothing left to hide. If I could have learned that at your age,

I would have walked in here tall, and on time this morning."

We sat in silence for a long time. Seemed like forever. I think we were both processing the conversation that had just taken place.

6

Dog Tags

My mind was spinning trying to process all that he just unloaded on me. As if he knew I was trying to put my thoughts in place, he got up to get another cup of coffee.

"You want another?"

"Maybe just some water."

As he made his way back to his chair, I noticed he wore a necklace of some kind. It appeared to be dog tags. I only recognized them because of all the war movies I've watched. As he sat back down, my curiosity once again took over as I heard myself blurt out, "Did you serve in the military?"

"Oh, these?" he said as he pulled the dog tags from underneath his shirt. "No, these belonged to my grandpa. I didn't really know him that well, but I have heard the stories of his heroic time spent in the United States Army. He was a bit of a local hero. He earned a bronze star and two purple hearts, among other things I have heard about. I wear these to remember where I come from and who I am."

"What do you mean who you are?" I asked feeling as though I might be getting another piece of wisdom long locked in his past.

"You see I was named after him."

Now I wished I had looked closer at the name on the tags, as I still didn't know his name.

"During times of war," he continued, "Soldiers wore these to identify themselves if they died in battle. I wear them as a reminder to be true to who I am. I wasted many years not knowing who I was. This life is sometimes like a war, and you can lose yourself if you're not careful."

We were on to something now. Remember the whole Superman had to know who he was so he could know what he was supposed to do thing? Once again, I was on the edge of my seat.

"I'm here to figure that very thing out!" I proclaimed.

How do you discover yourself? How do you know your identity? What's your purpose in life? My mind was racing! This could be the mother lode, I thought.

"Slow down young fellow!" he said. "You young guys are always in such a hurry. I was an old man before I discovered my identity. It took me a lifetime to excavate the real me."

"Had to take out some trash I suppose," I said trying to reinforce our previous talk.

"Oh yea! I filled up a dump. But under the trash of unforgiveness, I found me."

"I need to find me. I need my own dog tags. I am here trying to find my dad, hoping to fill in some blanks and better understand where I come from."

"You're on the right track," he said with encouragement. "I never took the time to find my dad. I felt if he wanted to meet me he would have found me. By the time I removed enough trash, he was dead and gone. I went to his funeral and that's where I got these dog tags. They belonged to his dad."

He continued, "Son, don't fall short on your journey. You find your dad. And when you do, more of your identity will be discovered, that will help you know your purpose. You see, I think dads are to help us discover our identity - what we are good at, what makes us unique. Maybe that has something to do with wearing their last name. Without his voice in our lives, many times we grow up having an identity crisis."

Feels like identity theft, I thought to myself.

"I have come to learn that it's our identity that leads us to the doorway of our destiny," he said.

"Wait! Say that again," I interrupted. "I need to write that down."

#4 Identity

"Our identity is the doorway to our destiny," he said again.

"That's why I met you!" I proclaimed, "If for no other reason, that's the jackpot of insight."

"Well, that other stuff was pretty good too, even if I do have to say so myself," he insisted. "I think we all have the potential of greatness, but accidents and hurt and disappointments, tragedies, abuse, abandonment, slowly rob us of our identity and we miss our doorway. Matter of fact, I was just watching a news report on identity theft and last year alone over ten million Americans were

> Our identity is the doorway to our destiny.

victims of identity theft. The cost was nearly fifty billion! Yet, what goes unreported is the millions who have their destiny stolen."

"So, what makes me, me?" I needed to know.

"Well, I can't tell you that. We just met. But maybe I can give you some clues. If you're anything like me, this will help. First of all, your genealogy, your DNA, the things you inherit, your height, skin color, the resistance, or even acceptance to diseases. Find out about your dad's health. It might give you clues to yours."

"Okay, that's good. But what else?"

"Birth order often has a lot to do with it. You're a first born, aren't you?"

"Yes," I replied. "How'd you know that?" I asked him.

"You can be a little bossy," he said. "First-borns like to tell others what to do. The good news is that they usually fill positions of authority and can be very self-motivated. Nobody told you to make this trip, did they?"

"Not at all," I said.

"I read somewhere that of the first 23 astronauts, 21 were first-borns. The other 2 were only children. Babies of the family are often comedians."

"Well, in that case, you must be a first born also, because you're not making me laugh," I said in jest.

"Guilty," he said, but without hesitation moved to the next clue. "Geography. Sounds odd, but where we live and grow up has some to do with who we are."

"Have you ever been in the South?" he asked, without giving me time to answer. "Sweet tea! Hey y'all! What about if you grow up in a communist country versus a free country, the inner city or the suburbs? All are pieces of the puzzle to who we become. That's not to mention the kind of people you hang out with. That's our sociology."

"Then, there is our theology, your concept of who God is," he announced. "I still don't know what I think about God. It seems like he could have been there for me when times were tough."

"Maybe he was," I interrupted. "Maybe we project the absence of our dads onto our ideas about God."

"Not a bad thought. I will have to think about that," he said.

I continued, "What about how I think about myself?"

"That would be your psychology," he said.

"Imagine your life as a Broadway play. Who do you want to be and what is the plot? Answer those questions and you will discover what you're passionate about. Choose some good supporting cast and a director here and there. Then open the curtain and let the drama begin. Shoot, you might even want to sell tickets," he laughed, reminding me that a good drama is filled with tragedy and comedy.

"I will be there for opening night," he said. "I think it will be a hit. The crowd might even sit on the edge of their seats. At times they will laugh, and other parts they will cry. We all will leave the theater a little better than we came in."

7

A Glass of Lemonade

Looking at his watch, he announced, "I am hungry how about you?"

"I guess I could eat something," I answered.

"The lunch crowd will be on this place like bees on honey soon," he announced.

I couldn't even believe that time had escaped us so fast. It seemed we just finished our morning coffee. Now, noon is knocking at the door, wanting to enter our conversation.

"I hear they have a good grilled ham and cheese sandwich here. What do ya say?" he asked.

"Sounds good to me," I said as I reached for my wallet.

"No, I got this one," he said. "It's the least I can do, for listening to me wade through all my baggage." With that, he made his way to the counter.

Wade through your baggage, I thought. This stuff is treasure! Where else can I get a front row seat, in a leather chair, and coffee, and lunch, and listen to an old man's lifetime of wisdom? I noticed the almost-high noon sun that was overtaking the morning and burning off the marine layer and had kept the morning so cold and gray, was now invading the coffee shop. Maybe it was the combination of the sun and the wisdom of the old sage that had me more hopeful than I had felt in a long time.

"Try this," he interrupted my thoughts. "The lady at the counter said they have the best lemonade in town. Thought it might go well with the sunshine," he said, as though he had the same appreciation for the sun's invasion of the coffee shop that was now making its reach known to the chairs we sat in.

"Probably the only lemonade," I said with a smile.

"I would like to propose a toast," I continued as he sat down again, and we raised our glasses of lemonade. "I declare that where I'm at is not where I have to stay, and that goes for you too."

"Cheers!" he said as we sat back to enjoy the warmth of the sun to drink our lemonade.

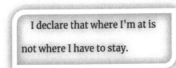
I declare that where I'm at is not where I have to stay.

"Wow! That's good lemonade," he proclaimed. I agreed.

"Funny thing about lemonade," he said. "It starts out as bitter sour lemons. If I was your age, I would drink more lemonade," he said. "I had plenty of lemons I just didn't know what to do with them all."

I knew I was ready to get another bomb of wisdom dropped on me, but was interrupted with a voice declaring, "Two ham and cheese sandwiches".

"That would be us," said the old man. "Hope they are as good as these lemonades."

"You like them?" the barista asked.

"Enough to add Tuesdays to my routine," he said.

"You're welcome here any day of the week," she said to him. With that she walked back behind him to bus a table, recently vacated, and looked back at me. Out of the old man's eyesight, she gave me a thumbs up with a big smile, as though she was celebrating a victory, like he finally said something other than his order to her. Seems like maybe everyone was winning today.

"Good sandwich, too," he called back to her, with his mouth still full of ham and cheese.

Yep, I thought. Breakthroughs all around. Halfway through our sandwiches the barista was back with a pitcher of lemonade and sat it on the table between us.

"Refills on the house today," she said.

I thanked her for her kindness. He nodded in agreement, as he had just taken another bite.

There wasn't much conversation as we finished our sandwiches, and then our glasses of lemonade. I grabbed the pitcher that looked as though it came from her grandma's house, filled our glasses again, and asked, "What was it you were saying about sour lemons?"

"I thought you forgot about that," he said. "I have lived long enough to know that life will serve you a lot of bitter lemons, and they can make you bitter, like I have become. Or, you can use them to make lemonade, and drink it with a friend. I wish I would have learned earlier that I can't tailor-make my circumstances, but I can tailor-make my attitude. It's really not what you go through, but how you go through it that matters. I spent so many negative years sucking on the bitter lemons of life. I have only recently come to realize that a positive attitude is one of the true choices I have left."

"Attitude determines your altitude," he continued. "It's not what we go through that really matters, it's how we go through it.

"Do you really believe you can control your attitude?" I asked. "What about when you get up on the wrong side of the bed?"

"Go back to bed and get out on the opposite side," he said with a grin. "I was angry yelling at my wife one time and the telephone rang. I grabbed it without even thinking and responded in the most pleasant tone you could ever imagine. That's choosing," he said with a tone of regret in his voice.

"I was just saying to you this morning to decide what character you want to play, like choosing to have a positive attitude and stick to the script. Stay true to the character you choose. I am only guessing, but I think life is 10 percent what happens to us and 90 percent how one reacts to it. A positive attitude also helps you get along with others better, and my success is largely determined by how I get along with others. I read once that the money you make on any endeavor is determined 12 percent by my knowledge and 88 percent by my ability to get along with other people."

Looking at his half glass of lemonade he asked, "Do you think this glass is half-empty or half-full?"

"I have heard this before," I said.

"Maybe there's another option," he said. "The optimist says the glass is half-full. The pessimist says its half-empty. Maybe the positive attitude just makes more lemonade and fills it up."

"So, the difference between an obstacle and an opportunity is my attitude?" I asked.

"I think you're onto something," he said. "The first time you saw me shuffle into this coffee shop, you viewed me as an obstacle, didn't you?

"Well I was...."

"It's okay, I get it," he interrupted, trying to ease my discomfort of the question.

"But now I see you as an opportunity," I quickly added.

"Exactly! What changed?" he inquired.

"My attitude," I said, as I imagined a bright light bulb hovering over my head.

"Yep. Problems, when you have a positive attitude, are only opportunities in work clothes. I think it was Thomas Edison who said, 'There are more opportunities than there are people to see them'."

He continued, "I made the mistake of thinking that the happy people in life were people that never went through hardships. I was wrong. Everyone has problems, and challenges. For example," he said as he was looking into space as if he was coming up with these illustrations on the fly. "If you bury a person in the snows of Valley Forge, you find George Washington. Raise him in poverty, and you have an Abraham Lincoln. Strike him down with paralysis, and he becomes a Franklin D. Roosevelt. Call him a slow learner and write him off as uneducable, and you have Albert Einstein. Fire him for not having any imagination, and you have Walt Disney."

"I get it," I said. "I choose. I choose to walk through this next challenge with a glass of lemonade in my hand," I proclaimed as I drank down my last swallow.

"Well said, grasshopper," he joked.

I suddenly realized that I wasn't writing and reached for my journal. The pages that had been blank for years were filling up with insight and wisdom that would otherwise take a lifetime to accumulate.

#5 Attitude, I wrote.

Then, in a serious tone he said, "You're going to be fine. Just don't let anyone or any circumstance have more power over you than your positive attitude. Remember to laugh and enjoy the journey. I sure wished I would have.

"I think I can do that. I will give it my best," I responded.

With that, he looked at his watch again and proclaimed, "Half our afternoon is now gone, and I still got chores to do at home. I best be get'n busy."

We both stood, and I stuck out my hand to shake his. "Thank you," I said. "You have given me a lot to think about." His hand in mine told another story. His hands were strong and calloused, they had never avoided work.

"You need any help with those chores?" I heard myself ask. I wasn't interested in doing chores as much as I was interested in digging up more of his treasured wisdom.

"No," he said. "I got nothing but time these days. I will get it done."

With that, he wished me good luck with my journey and we said our goodbyes. Maybe he could see disappointment in my eyes or maybe my company was a good change to his loner lifestyle. I'd like to think it was a little of both. He turned and said, "I tell ya what. If you can spare a little more time, you can come by my place in the morning. I have a coffee maker there. You will have to bring your own sugar though, I only drink mine…"

"Black!" I interrupted. "I will be there," I said, trying not to look overly excited. "Tell me the time and place."

"How about 8 AM? I will have the coffee on. Just go down this main street about three miles out of town," he said as he pointed out of town. "Take the first gravel road. There's a giant rock there. Head west. I am at the end of the road. It's the only house."

"I will be there," I confirmed. With that, he nodded and shuffled out to the sidewalk. I watched him climb into an old pickup truck that looked as old and worn out as he did. I stepped out on the sidewalk and watched him drive off, still trying to process the stories he told and this strong feeling of connection with this old man.

8

Lightning on the porch

The next morning couldn't come soon enough. I left the hotel far earlier than needed to make sure I could find his place. I passed the coffee shop on Main Street to see it coming to life, as it did the previous two mornings. Same faces, same stories. But not me. Not today. I was off to create a new chapter in my life. Three miles down the road, right at the big rock. I couldn't help but laugh out loud at the thought of it all.

There it is, the big rock just like he directed me. I slowly made the right turn. As I did, the morning sun was just peeking over the eastern mountain ridge to allow its glow into the valley and I could see its big orange glow in my rearview mirror. Maybe I was making more of it than I should, but it seemed an appropriate scene as to how I was feeling as I arrived at… Dandelion Acres? I noticed the big sign hanging over the gravel road that was evidently his driveway. 7:55 AM. The sun was awake and glimmering in the cockpit of my car and now glistening on the bright yellow field of dandelions. In the distance I could see an old house that seemed to be a football field away of nothing but yellow. I drove slowly as I was observing this amazing sunrise. Such a contrast to the morning of fog just 48 hours earlier.

I knew that he would expect me to be on time, and I didn't want to do anything that would compromise my time with him. As I reached the house, I was mesmerized. Other than the old pickup truck in the front and the old John Deere tractor out by the barn, it looked like something straight out of an old cowboy movie. Dandelions of yellow in the front, where it looked as though a garden or crop once grew, the water in the not too distant back and snow-capped mountains brought this painted picture all together. I could tell the place had seen its better days. As charming and picturesque as it was, it was old, worn out, and falling apart. I shouldn't I have expected anything else. Kind of seemed appropriate, as that was my evaluation of the old man when I first gazed upon his weathered appearance. The place was quiet, no motion. I hoped he remembered I was coming.

I put the car in park, grabbed my journal and emerged out of my car, which seemed a bit like a futuristic time machine in this setting. Closing the door loud enough to get his attention, I realized I had interrupted an old hound dog on the front porch, as though he was waiting for the morning sunlight to reach his place of sleep. I am sure he didn't see me as a threat as he barely acknowledged my presence. I had no sooner set foot on the porch, than the front screen door swung open and there stood the old man.

"Come on in! I got the coffee brewing," he proclaimed.

As I entered the house, he invited me to the kitchen to retrieve our coffee. The inside obviously lacked a woman's touch and was in keeping with the outside. It was clean, not a trace of trash, but definitely lived-in and plain. He grabbed the coffee pot and began to pour into the two cups he'd already set on the counter.

"Did you bring some sugar?" he asked.

"No, I decided to drink it black today. None of that sweet fu-fu stuff," I said, trying to be funny. He smiled as he handed me my cup of black coffee. He reached into the refrigerator to grab some homemade huckleberry jelly as four pieces of toast popped from the toaster.

Handing me two pieces of toast on a plate, and with coffee in hand, he led me to the den where he had a fire burning in the fireplace, complete with an elk mount above the mantle. We sat looking out over the property as the sun continued to illuminate the yellow acreage. I was trying to process all the items on the bookshelf to the side of him and noticed, decorated amongst the books, where three little Tonka trucks like the ones I had grown up with, served as a reminder as to the reason for my being here.

"How long have you lived here?" I asked.

"35 years! Bought the place when I was 48. I used to have a ranch hand that helped me take care of this place," he said as he gazed out across his land.

That must have been a long time ago I thought, as I observed a property with overgrown fruit trees, broken fences, and an empty chicken coop.

"I used to raise animals for food and grow my own fruits and vegetables," he stated. "Not much living here anymore except some weeds, me and Lightning," he continued.

"Lightning?" I asked.

"Yeah, my guard dog on the front porch," he said, with a sarcastic smirk on his face.

"How long since you've had any help around here?" I asked.

"Hershel died of a heart attack about 5 years ago," he said. "I hired him when I was in my late sixties to help me keep this place running. He was with me for about 10 years. He became a pretty good friend in that time. Your gonna need that in your life,"

"What's that?" I inquired.

"Friends," he replied. "I called him Hercules. He was a mountain of a man. He could work harder than anyone I've ever known. The first year he was here he would follow me as I would plow the field and pick up the rocks. That old yellow field used to be as green as a lime. Hercules would take weed killer and walk every step spraying those old dandelions. Can't get rid of them by mowing. You gotta get to the roots. Roots and rocks. I guess you could say that was his job description. I would have had to sell this old place if it hadn't been for him. He sang and whistled as he worked, it used to get on my nerves how anyone could be that happy all the time.

The old man continued, "Sometimes when I am out mowing the field, I still think I can hear him. I sure do miss that old guy. I wished I would have learned the value of friendship sooner. This old place might be in better shape." I was looking out the wall of windows with him as he made the statement I assumed he was talking about the property, only to look over at him just in enough time to notice he was patting himself on the chest as he made that statement.

"This old ranch was alive and well, when Hercules was around helping. Back then, Lightning was younger, and the huckleberry bushes were still providing jelly for my morning toast."

"Come to think of it," he said, "I think a man needs all three."

I wasn't quite following.

"Three levels of friends," he said.

Okay, somewhere I missed it, I thought. Instead of appearing slower than I was, I allowed him to continue, thinking I would catch up.

"You gonna need some Hercules, Hound Dogs, and Huckleberry," he said with the inspiration of an old southern preacher. "Hercules are stronger or smarter than you in some area that you need to grow in, and they will fight for whatever you're against. They are the friends in life that will get in the trenches and fight the things that you are trying to overcome, and if you're gonna overcome, you're gonna need a Herculean friend that can help lift what you can't lift by yourself."

Like the old brass bell ringing in the coffee shop, the bell in my brain kicked in as I suddenly got what he meant.

"Now Hound Dogs, they are a different story," he said as he leaned forward to see old Lightning still laying on the porch. "They are the friends that will be with you because of what you're after in life. They share the same interests, passions, and pursuits. You tell them what you're trying to accomplish, the goals, and dreams in your life, and they will do everything in their power to help you reach that destination."

He looked at the elk above the fireplace, "I could have never shot big Al if I didn't have a Hound Dog. And I am not talking about Lightning," he quickly said. Not allowing me to respond he continued, "Next, if you're lucky, you have one or two Huckleberries in your life. They are like bridge builders," he said.

"Wait, what did you just say?" I interrupted.

"They are like bridge builders. They help you get where you're going. They will help you in the gaps of life, like a bridge over troubled water," he said.

I was having another connect the dot light bulb moment.

"Look for them. Invest in them," he schooled me. "They are the kind of folks that will hang with you no matter what. You will need to stand on their shoulders from time to time to reach higher than you can alone. They don't care what you're for or against, they are just with you. They will see you at your worst, but still believe the best in

> True friends can step on your toes without messing up your shine.

you. They keep you honest. They can step on your toes without messing up your shine," he said with a smile, as he ate his last bite of huckleberry toast. With that he asked me if I wanted another cup of coffee.

"I sure do," I replied as he took my cup with his and headed to the kitchen whistling the theme to Huckleberry Hound, and I couldn't help but think that maybe our conversation was doing him as much good as it was doing for me.

While he was in the kitchen I grabbed my journal, turned to the first blank page and wrote:

#6 Friends

9

Pink elephants

As he entered the den with two fresh cups of coffee, he continued to speak as if it was a postscript to the conversation, picking up as though there hadn't been a break.

"Look to be that kind of friend to someone and look for someone to be that to you. It's like iron sharpening iron," he said as he handed me my cup.

"If each man would find a way to serve another man, we could get so much farther along in life. I think we spend so much time pulling people down to our level that we don't have anyone to look to when we want to go up a level. If I were living my life over, I would live with an open circle. I wouldn't shut people out. Who knows? The people you shut out could be the very people to help you. Acceptance doesn't have to mean agreement. If you wait until you agree with everyone about everything before allowing them into your circle of friendship, you will end up like me. Alone!" he said with the tone of a judge lowering his gavel.

We sat for a few minutes in silence, allowing me to process what he had just said.

Breaking the silence, he questioned me, "What are you doing here?"

"To help you with chores," I responded.

"But why?" he asked again. "You told me you were out here to meet your dad. Why are you here wanting to help an old man with his chores?"

"I guess I am a bit nervous, so I'm procrastinating. Not to mention I've enjoyed our time together. I guess I am trying to find my own set of dog tags," I admitted.

"Yep! Procrastination is one of the first symptoms of fear. It's not bad to be afraid. Courage isn't the absence of fear. You can't have courage without fear."

"I plan on facing my fear tomorrow," I said.

"Spoken like a true procrastinator," he said with a laugh. "You still want to help me with some chores?"

"Sure, I'd be glad to," I said, feeling as though he had something else up his sleeve.

"Well, you see those dandelions out there? The spring rains really bring them up in full force," he said.

How could I miss them, I thought?

"I need to mow that field today, while the sun is out. Maybe while I mow you can help me by picking up the dead branches around the yard and the old fruit trees and help me make a burn pile," he said. "There are some pruning shears and gloves in the barn."

"You sure you can spare a couple hours for chores?" he asked.

"I am your huckleberry," I replied.

He laughed and stood to lead the way out to the barn where the tractor was parked. He slowly climbed up on the old faded green tractor and turned the key. A few spit and sputters later, the old thing came to life as though she was coming out of a long winter hibernation. He made his way slowly off the tractor and to the barn door. As the door rolled open, the outside sun quickly overtook the darkness to shine in areas that I am certain hadn't seen daylight in a very long time, revealing what seemed more like a time capsule. My initial observation unraveled more of the old man's story. There it sat. A double-winged airplane covered in years of dust.

The fact than an old airplane sat in his barn gave a little more credibility to the statement he had made the day before: *your attitude determines your altitude.* I think he knew I was having another connecting the dots moment as I caught him watching me observe the airplane. Without offering any explanation regarding why he had an airplane, he made his way toward the back of the barn to retrieve some work gloves. I tried to follow him, only to slow down as I observed slack-jawed, the diversity of things held hostage in the old barn. There, in the corner, was an old Harley that by the looks of it had long since seen any highway. Or how about the boat, that I know hasn't been in the water for who knows how long? The old car, tractor parts, and plenty of tools, much of which I don't think has seen work in many years. As I was gawking at the contents of this old barn, he handed me some gloves and pointed me in the direction of all the yard tools.

"Before you start your chores, I want you to do something for me," he said.

"Ok. I'll try," I responded.

"Stop thinking about pink elephants," he said.

"I wasn't thinking about them until you mentioned them," I argued.

"Exactly," he said. "Too many times we spend our mental energy thinking about what we shouldn't, leaving us without mental horsepower to think about what we should. It's very difficult to chase the wrong thoughts out of our mind unless we can fill the void with the thoughts of good possibilities."

"I want you to think about what you want your meeting to look like with your dad. I want you to think about what your relationship might look like. I want you to paint the picture in your mind of everything you hope for. Stop letting pink elephants trample your picture. Ignore all the fearful thoughts. Most of the things you worry about won't happen anyway," he said with a conviction that only experience can dictate.

"I am convinced that what you think about in life is where you go about," he declared.

As he made that statement he looked up and pointed at some geese flying back north. "You

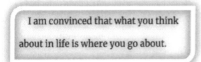

I am convinced that what you think about in life is where you go about.

see those geese?" he asked.

"Sure, I do," I answered.

"You can't help the fact that birds fly over your head, but you can keep them from building a nest in your hair. In other words, we all have negative thoughts pass through our minds. The key is not to dwell on them. Don't dwell on the negative possibilities. Pour a big glass of lemonade, and dwell on the positive possibilities."

He continued, "Many times, success is determined by the size of our thinking and we have to determine what we will think about. Changing your thinking will change your vocabulary. Painting the picture in your mind of what you want it to look like changes what we see, from what it is, to what can be. Positive thinking releases creativity and excitement."

"Why are you nervous about meeting your dad?" he asked.

"I guess I am afraid of what to even say," I answered.

"Then, think about it. Think through what you will talk about. If I may be so bold as to say that you are nervous because you have listened too long to the lies in your own head. Your mind has been trained to say you're not accepted. So, while your cutting and pruning branches, prune your thoughts and every thought that has been allowed to grow wild, like them old trees. Cut it out and replace it with true, positive thinking and I bet you will get some pretty good fruit in the days and years to come."

"Now, it takes me about two hours to mow, he informed me, as he climbed back onto the tractor. "I want you to imagine all the great things that can come out of your meeting. Think about all the positive conversations you can have. Imagine his questions to you and yours to him."

With that being said, he put the old tractor in gear and made his way to the sea of yellow dandelions.

As I watched him drive away, he faded into a small green spot and began erasing one row of yellow at time. I made my way to the fruit trees to begin pruning untamed branches, picking up dead branches and dragging them to the burn pile, then cutting them to fit within the radius of ashes that had previously been established by a parameter of rocks that would keep the fire contained. I was not only pruning trees, but pruning the thoughts that had lied to me for years. Lies that I believed, thoughts that said he didn't want me or didn't care about me, and wondering how I ever let those thoughts grow so strong. I realized I didn't know his circumstances. I had let false imagination grow to a level that only produced fruit of fear, rejection, and insecurity. It was time to control my thoughts, because what I think about is where I go.

The fire was well underway, crackling and consuming the branches that had once cluttered the yard. I acted as if every branch I threw in the fire was a negative thought that had lied to me with intentions of keeping me from my purpose. Two hours had come and gone, and I was still cutting and burning branches. I was lost in thought - positive, truthful thoughts, that had me looking forward to my meeting, and feeling like I don't think I have ever felt. The fear and negativity seemed to burn away like the branches in the fire.

I hadn't even noticed the yellow field was now green and the tractor was parked. He had completed his mission of mowing. My mission, still unfinished had really only just begun. Two hours had quickly become three as I filled my last wheelbarrow full of branches. I was completely lost in my thoughts and enjoying the smell of fresh cut grass, and the smoke from the burning branches. As though he were waiting for me to complete my task, he emerged from the house with a glass of lemonade.

"Take a load off," he said as he handed me a glass, then pulled up a log to sit by the fire.

"Thank you," he said. "You've been a big help."

I sat with him and wiped the sweat from my forehead while examining newly earned blisters. Not realizing that the smoke of the fire found a resting place on my face, leaving behind a black tint, it provided clear evidence of the trail of tears that had run down my cheeks while imagining a relationship with my dad that was long overdue. We sat in silence by the remaining fire, both of us appreciating the work we had just accomplished.

10

That's Not Your Problem

"The yard looks great!" I said, finally breaking the silence.

"Yeah, but it will be yellow again by tomorrow," he said. "Unless you kill the roots."

"Kinda like taking out the trash, huh," I piped in.

"For sure, but a little more painful," he replied. "While I was mowing, I was thinking about facing the fear."

"Yeah?" I replied.

"Well," he continued, "There isn't any shame in having a problem, or having fears, although none of us like to admit that we have them."

With that, he handed me my journal that I had left in the den and said, "I think this will be worth writing down." I quickly wrote down...

#7 Positive Thinking

Somehow, I felt as though he was passionate about what he was getting ready to share, as though he wished someone had given him this advice when he was younger.

"Your problem is not your problem. How you handle your problem is the real problem, and not everything is a problem."

"Did you get that?" he asked.

"I'm writing," I responded.

#8 Face Your Fears

"You see we all have problems, though they come dressed in different clothes. The difference between success and failure is how we solve our problems. I am sitting here giving you advice. But in reality, you are solving your problem. You're asking questions and you're out here searching for him."

Then he hung his head and said, "I never searched. I've lived with that problem for all these years," he said with much regret in his voice.

Then with renewed passion he proclaimed, "You don't have to. You're attempting to solve the problem. I was taking my own advice while I was mowing and thinking about the problem you face and what I have learned. It's a mistake to leave a job, a marriage, or any relationship because of a problem. Unresolved relationship problems only resurface in the next relationship. Take it from me; problems don't disappear if they are ignored. Ignored problems don't go away, they just get older, and gain strength. Problems can propel us forward if we respond to them the way you are trying to."

"How's that?" I asked.

"You're facing them," he replied. "A problem should never leave us the same. You've made me realize that the size of the person is more important than the size of the problem."

"Wow! Now he's learning from me. I didn't even know I was teaching," I said with a smile.

He laughed and continued, "You have a big problem because you have a big goal. Small plans will always attract small problems, like big plans will always attract big problems. Don't let the size of your problems dictate the size of your plans. Don't allow things that don't propel you toward your goals to become problems. A problem is something that stands in your way of a better outcome, so don't waste your time and energy trying to fight every battle or solve every problem. If you keep in mind what you're fighting for, you will have the stamina to face the problem for as long as it takes to get the job done."

"Did you see that old boat in the barn?" he asked.

"Yes," I responded.

"Well, when I first started taking it out on the water, I realized one day that the main problem or obstacle that the boat faces is the water that is applying pressure and resistance to the propeller. Yet. if it were not for that resistance, the boat would not move."

> Don't waste your time and energy trying to fight every battle or solve every problem.

"Problems can be wake up calls to creativity. Sometimes to connect the dots, you have to think outside the box," he said.

I was writing things down as fast as I could. He looked down at my journal and said "Draw three dots across the top of that page, then three more right under them. Now, three more under them, he instructed. "Now, connect the dots without retracing any or lifting your pen."

He watched me try a few times then said, "If you're going to solve the problem and connect the dots, you have to draw outside the lines."

And that was what I needed - permission to face the fear, to think outside the box! Dots connected, problem solved.

11

Old Winchester

I kicked back in my folding chair with a feeling of accomplishment. Not just the burning of branches, but I felt as though I was preparing myself for the rest of my life. We both gazed into the remaining embers of the fire as the sun moved to the west and lit up the snow-capped mountains in the distance that hovered over his property like walls around a city.

"Have you ever been up there?" I asked him.

"Only once. It's not an easy task, but I should've climbed it more. It's a beautiful sight from up there. I should have climbed a lot of mountains. I am too old now," he said with a sigh.

"But you - you have some mountains to climb. You have a dream to have a relationship with your dad, right?" he asked.

"Yes. That's why I'm here."

"Your dream is like that mountain. The question is, what are you doing about it, today?" he asked.

Before I could answer, he continued, "I know something about every person who has stood on the top of that mountain."

"What's that?" I asked.

"They didn't fall there, and they didn't get there by accident. The same is true for reaching our dreams. It will take planning, sacrifice and determination. But the view of a fulfilled dream is worth the climb," he said as though he was reminiscing about the view from the top.

> The view of a fulfilled dream is worth the climb.

"You're going to have to break your dreams into goals," he continued.

The puzzled look on my face must have tipped him off to continue the thought.

"A goal is a dream with a deadline. I always had good intentions but I never broke things down or put them on my daily calendar. If you're going to accomplish anything great, then you must do something about it every day. Every day check your goals, and then check your actions and behavior to make sure they match. You will always know you're on the road to success because it will be uphill all the way."

He seemed to be on a roll and wisdom that had been birthed by his own procrastination and regret was coming out at full throttle. I was writing notes as fast as I could as he continued as though if he paused he would lose his thought.

"There's a lot of dreamers out there. They talk much, but accomplish very little. But a dream broken down into goals and put on your calendar, well, that's a different story. It's as if you get a hold of the dream, then the dream gets a hold of you."

"Climbing that mountain gave me a great feeling of accomplishment, like it did me a favor. Dreams do the same," he said.

"I am not sure I follow," I admitted.

"The dream begins to serve you and mold you. Dreams will also provide needed direction. I lived too much of my life reactive and not proactive, like an octopus on roller skates, going wherever direction that circumstances take me," he said with another sigh of regret.

"If you don't have a dream, you will wander through life. If you have a dream, but don't pursue it, then you will wonder about it all your life. I also think that a dream will keep you motivated. When I climbed that mountain, I was tired and wanted to quit half way up. But I was motivated to reach the top. One of the biggest motivation killers in life is not knowing why you are doing what you are doing. If you don't have a reason to get out of bed in the morning, you probably won't. You must keep in mind what it will look like if you reach the top. What will it look like if you climb your own mountain? What could it look like to have a relationship with your dad?"

"The dream will give you energy," he continued. as I thought for sure my hand would cramp up from trying to write all this down.

"I once read a story about a lady named Florence Chadwick," he recalled. "In 1964, she wanted to be the first lady to swim from the Catalina Islands over to the coast of California. That's twenty-four miles, if I remember right. The day was foggy and after 15 hours of swimming, she gave up only a little way from the coast. A reporter asked her why she didn't finish. Her reply has haunted me to this day," he said as he looked away from the mountain and straight into my eyes.

"What was her response?" I asked.

"She said, 'I couldn't see the coast.' That's why you gotta keep your dreams alive in your mind."

"Yeah, if you can see it, you can seize it, right?" I asked. remembering his statement from the first day we met.

"You're a fast learner," he said with a smile.

After these last couple thoughts, he was now approaching preacher status, as though my life or his was depending on this information.

He looked at me with an intense resolve and said, "Whatever you do, don't give up on your dreams when life looks boring or ordinary. That's where I always got off track. I have come to realize that extra-ordinary days are made up of a lot of ordinary days. There are no shortcuts to anyplace worth going. You will usually get less than you expect in one year, but more than you expect in five years.

"If I was to guess," he said, "I think reaching your goals, like climbing that mountain, is 1 percent inspiration and 99 percent perspiration. The truth is, I wanted to climb that mountain again, but I let it intimidate me. So, I procrastinated, and it beat me. But remember, dreams don't crumble when we fail. The dream crumbles when we surrender."

He continued, "I am an old man filled with regret, and wishful thinking of things I should've done. I sit here in the twilight of my days wishing I had some years and energy to add to the wisdom that could have come through hope and discipline, but I chose, through indecision, to gain through regret and misplaced steps. Get out there! Live the life you hope for! Go climb your mountains!"

"The best thing I can do for you is say goodbye. Go call your dad and begin to grab a hold of the things you are hoping for, or else you will end up like me - a grumpy old man alone on a ranch with memories of what could have been."

12

Good-Bye Old Man, Hello Dad

The sun was now beginning to set over the very mountain that had become the backdrop for my last bit of wisdom from the old man. I knew our time was coming to an end and I could feel the cool night air beginning to overtake the warmth of this spring day that had accomplished so much. Inch by inch, the sun was disappearing, not to be found again until its dawn, marking the beginning of a new day's journey. I knew it was time to say goodbye, but I was procrastinating again. If I was to take his advice, I dare not ask any more questions or gather more information. It was time to act. I closed my journal as though

I was closing this unique chapter that had mysteriously unfolded over the last three days.

"Thank you," I managed to say. "Thanks for the insight and advice."

"You can thank me by getting out of here and redeem some of my mishaps and mistakes," he snarled, obviously trying not to get emotional. "I will die with the peace of knowing that my mistakes have helped someone get a little closer to the top of their mountain. Maybe something that I said will keep you from living alone with constant reminders that continually haunt you with regret and remind you of a life you could have and should have lived."

"Live your life. Don't let life live you. That's how you can thank me," he continued.

I wasn't certain if he was pushing me away or motivating me to get started, so I took the hint and stood to my feet and asked if I would ever see him again.

"You never know," he said. "I am 83. My time is getting close."

"I hope you will see me in your mind," he said with a bit of a softer tone. "Every time you climb a mountain and stand on its shoulders viewing a sunset. I hope you will think of me every time you take out the trash or drink a glass of lemonade or eat some huckleberry toast. You got 60 years of living to catch up to me. Make the most of them. Make every day count. The decisions you make on any given subject won't make

> Live your life. Don't let life live you.

or break you. It's all the little decisions you make after the big decision is made that determines your success."

"Now go meet your dad and let that be the first step to a life filled with amazing journeys. Live your life like the character you want to be. The world is your stage. I think you are going to be fine. In my mind I will be front row and I will see you after the play."

With that he reached out, shook my hand and covered it with his other, and looked me straight in the eye and said in a desperate tone, "Remember you don't have to be great to start something, but you have to start to be great. Now, go get started. I am counting on you!"

Feeling a bit awkward and confused by his last comment, I didn't want to overstay my welcome. I managed to say goodbye as I walked to my car that was now beginning to collect the dew of the evening air. I opened the door and noticed that the movement had Lightning looking up at me as if to say goodbye. This morning, the sun was rising on our day when I arrived and now it was gone. I got to the end of the driveway to turn toward my hotel and I could still see the orange glow now barely visible from the fire. I was surprised how emotional I was. I only knew the old man for three days, yet I was saddened to say goodbye and excited for the sun to rise on tomorrow. Before pulling onto the road I wrote...

#9 Dream

As I drove through the town towards my hotel, I couldn't get his last words out of my mind. They hovered in my mind like the morning fog that often settled in this town, almost haunting me.

I arrived at my room and ordered some room service, determined not to let my day end without doing something about my tomorrow while it was still today. I picked up the phone and dialed a number that was very familiar to me as I had imagined dialing it thousands of times. My heart was beating hard as I could hear it in the receiver of the phone. Feel the fear and do it anyway I thought to myself. Four rings, should I leave a message? Or call back? I will wait one more....

"Hello?" I heard his voice say, not realizing that one hello would echo the introduction of a whole new life for me.

"Hello, Dad. This is your son."

"Who?" he asked, activating an adrenaline rush and an urge to hang up.

"It's your son. I was hoping we could talk."

"You're kidding? I have been hoping for this day for years! I am so glad you called," he said.

"I'm in your area and I was really hoping you could take some time to get together."

"Name the time and place and I'll be there."

When I told him where I was, he interrupted and said, "There is a great little coffee shop there, I like to stop in as often as possible. I can meet you there first thing in the morning, if that works for you," he said.

"I know right where it's at," I answered. "I would love to meet you for coffee."

"How's tomorrow at 8 sound to you?" he asked.

"Perfect," I said trying not to sound overly anxious. "I'll see you then."

"I'll be driving a blue mustang, so you can recognize me, as we have both changed a little over the years," he said.

"Good idea! And I will be wearing a black Harley Davidson hoodie," I said. And with that, we said our goodbyes.

It felt so strange to hear his voice, knowing that I was just hours away from achieving a dream. I didn't sleep much that night. Make believe conversations danced through my thoughts as I practiced what the old man had told me. Imagine the positive outcome. What you think about is where you go about…

I had questions, but I didn't want him to feel like I was interrogating him. So many questions. Did he think of me? Does he have other kids? Did he miss me? Why didn't he ever call? I wondered if he remembered the Tonka truck roads in the backyard.

My mind was racing, as I watched each minute click by like it was a second hand. I felt like a kid on Christmas Eve.

The morning finally arrived, and I jumped up to get ready, making sure to put on my black Harley Davidson hoodie. I practically ran to the coffee shop. As I walked, I noticed that the morning fog was back. It wasn't so thick that you couldn't see, but thick enough to reveal only the silhouette of people and places unable to find enough detail to reveal their full identity. As I approached the town clock one block from the coffee shop, I noticed the little hand was on the 8 and the big hand was on the 10. I wanted to be early, so I could watch for him. I wanted to avoid the embarrassment of not recognizing him or him not recognizing me for that matter.

The last few yards to the coffee shop seemed as though they were happening in slow motion. It was all so surreal. Walk tall, I heard the old man's voice echo in my mind. Recalling our previous conversations, you have nothing left to prove and nothing left to hide. With my next step I could see what looked like a man leaning on a car. Was that him? Next step, he looked my way and stood up, that must be him. The next step put me only feet away and my black hoodie and his blue mustang were in clear sight, yet somehow, we didn't need the props to recognize each other. The search had come to an end as he made a move towards me.

"Son? Is that you?"

"Hi Dad. It's me."

Before I could get the words out of my mouth, I felt myself in an embrace that was 20 years overdue. Somehow, many of the questions I had worried about and lost sleep over were answered. It felt as though time stood still. I couldn't believe how the words 'Son, I missed you,' seemed to answer so many questions and heal so many wounds. It seemed like a strange time to think about it, but I couldn't help but think of the old man. I felt sorry for him. I felt sorry that he never went looking for his dad and would never experience what I was experiencing at that moment.

"Thanks for finding me," my dad said with an obvious lump in his throat. "I have dreamed of this day for years. I lost track of where you guys were and wondered if I would ever hear from you or see you again."

If I hadn't taken out the trash a few days before, I might not have been prepared to hear that statement. Hearing that without resentment or bitterness in my heart allowed me to grab his words like a lost treasure.

"That's all in the past, as far as I am concerned. How about we get in out of the cold, get some coffee and start working on the future," I said.

"Sounds good to me," he said as I opened the door, and once again heard the little brass bell announce. Father and son have just entered the room together.

"Can I help you?" the barista asked my Dad.

"I will take a white chocolate Americano," he said.

I laughed to myself and said, "Make that two."

We sat facing the window as we drank our coffee and made small talk about life in general and traveled down memory lane a bit. As we talked, I noticed the sun had once again burned off some morning fog and was now illuminating the east side of that snow-capped mountain.

"That's Winchester mountain," my dad mentioned.

"Have you ever been to the top?" I asked.

"Funny you should ask that," he said with a puzzled look on his face. "I was in town last Monday picking up some parts for the shop. It was another foggy morning typical in the spring, much like today. I stopped in for a coffee and as I was standing looking out this same window, I took my first drink and an old man passed me and asked how I was doing. Just another ordinary day, I responded."

An old man? Last Monday! I was thinking, trying not to bust out an interrupt, while maintaining my composure.

"Then he asked me the same question that you just asked me," he said. "'Have I ever been to the top of that mountain?' I responded, 'no, but I always wanted to.' 'Do it!' The old man said to me. I was a little blown away at how bold and demanding he seemed."

I know what you mean I thought to myself.

"What did he say then?" I asked.

"The old man told me 'That if I always do what I have always done, then I will always get what I have always had. I don't know where you're at in life,' the old man said, 'but wherever you're at is not where you have to stay. Trade in some ordinary days for some extra-ordinary days. If you string too many ordinary days together you will end up like me, an old man with a lot of extra-ordinary regrets. I dare ya to go hike that mountain and take someone with you, someone that needs to over-come an obstacle or reach a goal. It will change your

> If I always do what I have always done, then I will always get what I have always had.

perspective. When you reach the top, have some lem-onade and enjoy what you have done.' With that, the old man walked out into the fog and that was it."

He is kinda like that, I was thinking to myself.

"That's my long way of saying that I have never been to the top, but I have been thinking about get-ting up there while I am still able," he said.

"We should hike it together!" I heard myself blurt out and confessed I had met the same old man.

"Maybe the old man is on to something," I said, "Even if he was a bit grumpy and direct."

"You can say that again," my dad responded.

"What did he say to you?" my dad questioned me.

"Well, mostly just chit-chat, some other things I can share with you on the hike," I said with a bit of a question mark, feeling for the first time in years like a little boy wanting to hang out with his dad.

"And he did recommend the lemonade," I said with a smile.

PART 3
The Reveal

"Challenging circumstances do not decide who I am, they can only reveal who I already was."

Ken Hubbard

13

Full Circle at 7000 ft

The morning air was very crisp as we arrived at the trailhead of Winchester Mountain the next morning. It stood tall and proud, a bit intimidating, yet inviting at the same time. We had finished the previous day getting me checked out of the hotel and into his place. Then, we went boot and supply shopping. I still couldn't believe I was about to spend the next two days hiking with my dad.

"There is a fire lookout at the top," Dad said. "We will hike to the top by this evening and spend the night in the lookout, that is if the snow doesn't get too deep."

Hiking mountains, camping, and spending time with my dad is all new territory for me. But the old man had me determined to face my fears, climb my mountains, and already I could feel my life changing for the better.

One step at a time, I thought to myself. I'm sure getting to the top would prove more challenging and exhausting than I could ever imagine. The thought of having my dad's full attention, just the two of us together, climbing, hiking, and catching up had me discovering my own nugget of wisdom. I wasn't as interested in getting to the top of the mountain as I was interested in enjoying the time with him. Maybe it's not always about the destination, but more about the journey in life.

> Maybe it's not always about the destination, but more about the journey in life.

I thought that the five-mile trip to the top wouldn't be a big of a deal, until an hour later we had barely reached the one-mile mark. Our conversation kept my mind occupied, though I found it challenging at times to hike and talk at the same time without running out of breath. Dad did a lot of the talking about where he had been and what his life had looked like over the past 20 years with familiar tones of regret that I had heard from the old man, laid heavy on the stories of his life. I resolved that I would avoid regret at all cost. I would rather hike mountains and have blisters from new boots than to get old with regrets of what mountains I could have climbed.

Somewhere about the halfway point I noticed that the thick forest began to thin out and the trees were sparse and small. This provided a view like I had never experienced. My dad, knowing the area, began to point out other places that we could now see.

"There's Mt. Baker," he said, telling me stories of fishing on Baker Lake. "There's the Canadian Rockies to our left and over there on Slide Mountain is where I used to go hunting."

We found a nice place to rest and break out some lunch, so we climbed onto a giant boulder that looked like it had rolled from the top hundreds of years ago. We had reached the elevation that put us above the clouds allowing the afternoon sun to warm us as we sat together. And for the first time since we met, there was silence. No words needed to be spoken.

I think we were both lost in the moment, a moment that we had both longed for. The cruel obstacles that had kept us apart were now being climbed and overcome like this very mountain we were hiking together on. If I could capture the feelings in a bottle from that moment, I would be a rich man. If the old man could see me now! Talk about connecting dots - I think it might even put a smile on his face.

I felt like a little boy again, but it was okay. It was healing some broken parts that had been left unattended for many years. It's hard to explain, but the more I embraced being a kid, the more I felt like a man. Ready to leap tall buildings in a single bound... no. But, I felt able to hike tall mountains one step at a time, overcoming the obstacles that had delayed my journey more times than I care to admit.

We sat there for more than an hour. I think he took a little nap as I pulled my journal from my backpack and sketched the peaks of the mountains that were in view, trying to capture a memory and a feeling that I didn't ever want to escape my mind. It was mid-afternoon when we decided to continue up the trail. We were at the elevation and the time of year when the snow began to appear and cover what had been an easy trail to follow.

"It's gonna get a little slower from this point on," he said to me. "Make sure to dig your foot into every step. The last mile is always the hardest."

Every step had slowed to a pace that allowed the conversation to catch up the years that had been lost. Each step a dot. Each story a line. I was able to see things more clearly from here than ever.

"There's the fire lookout," Dad proclaimed.

We are close now. We stopped only to get a drink and for him to caution me on my footing. One foot in front of the other. One step at a time. My legs were on fire! But the thrill of reaching the top was greater that the exhaustion or the sore feet.

As we arrived at the summit, we high-fived each other, both knowing there was more to this than a simple hike. Dad dropped his gear and began to open the lookout cabin that was sitting on the very top of the mountain. The cabin was reinforced by cables that stretched out like tent cords and driven into giant boulders that led to Winchester's peak. Opening the shutters allowed the evening sun to warm the small square room, furnished with a pot belly stove and two bunks that looked like shelves hanging from the wall.

We unloaded our gear and built a fire. Windows on all sides allowed a 360-degree view of the mountains and an appreciation for the journey. I kicked off my boots allowing my feet to escape their painful prison. My feet were sore, and my body was tired. But my heart was full. It seems like nothing hurts when you've fulfilled a dream. I felt as if I was on top of the world.

"I have a surprise for you," Dad said as he pulled two bottles of lemonade out of his backpack and handed me one.

We kicked back to enjoy our victory, letting the sun hit our faces. The crackling of the fire and the melting of snow from the sun's warmth could be heard cascading into waterfalls making their way down to the river much faster than we made our way up to the lookout. The orange glow of the sun that was now setting over peeks to the west reminded me of the campfire where I sat with the old man just two days before. If he only knew how thankful I was for his advice. I wished he could see me now. I was there, drinking lemonade at the top of old Winchester with my dad.

We sat and watched as the sky changed from orange to purple. The shade of purple got darker and darker, until eventually it was black. We never slept that night. We talked and shared while we kept the fire alive. I filled him in on the childhood of mine that he had missed. I lost all track of time, but somewhere in the night's conversation by the glow of the fire, he looked at me and asked me to forgive him for not being there. Every hurt that had held me hostage through the years had to release me from what could have been a life sentence as I assured my dad that all was forgiven. I would never dwell on the past, only focus on the future.

"Thank you, son" he said. "I love you and I am proud of the man that you have become."

I'm proud of you echoed in my mind, never knowing that would be the catalyst for my identity and the beginning of a whole new purpose for me. I couldn't believe how fast the night had come and gone. We were still enjoying our conversation and catching up when I noticed the little cabin begin to fill with the morning light. It's a new day I thought to myself. I felt as though that one night brought closure and with one chapter now closing, another could begin. I had come full circle at 7,000 ft.

14

I Blinked

More often than not, the sand goes through the hourglass too fast, and even faster since that day with Dad at the lookout. Not a day goes by that I don't think about the lessons I learned in a conversation with a stranger. Nine days: three days with the old man, and six days with my dad. I feel like the trajectory of my whole life changed in those nine days. I've since lost track of the notes I wrote in that old journal, but I think of the conversations often - principles and wisdom gleaned from an old man filled with regret and loneliness.

I often hear his voice reminding me to *walk tall*, *the world is your stage*, and *face your fear*. I think about him every time I serve my kids a glass of lemonade on a hot summer day.

I am not sure how things would have turned out if I hadn't of bumped into that old timer. I am pretty sure I wouldn't have mustered the courage to find my dad. Since that time, I've made many memories as I traveled back and forth on many occasions, sometime alone and sometimes with my wife and two kids. I do my best to live a life without regrets, like the old man warned me. It's my way of thanking him, for the nine life lessons that changed everything.

Those lessons became my life map, and for countless others who would take time to grab a coffee with me and allow me to share the nine lessons that I learned. I am sure there were some who thought the list was too long. Others probably thought the list was too short, or maybe even some thought the list should be different. Maybe so. But they are the nine that were told to me, birthed from the hurts and regrets of an old man who desperately would have loved a second chance at this thing we call life. When I share these nine with others, I imagine the old man sitting there with me. I can almost hear him repeating with me...

1. Forgiveness - Take out the Trash

The day I sat in the coffee shop filled with anxiety and fear was largely due to the trash and unforgiveness that I unknowingly allowed to imprison me. I realized that hurts, disappointments, and negative words of others had polluted my soul. I needed a detox. I needed to take out the trash and continue taking it out. Otherwise, bitterness and regret would have strangled my dreams, just like those of the old man.

Unforgiveness was fueling the shame that, at that time, I didn't even realize had hitched a ride in my life. Shame had been quietly residing in the shadows of unforgiveness and had almost convinced me that I was not good enough to pursue my dreams. The old man wasted his years believing the lie of shame. Heeding his stern and passionate advice to take out the trash and forgive myself and those who hurt me began to silence the intimidating, relentless voice of shame.

I once heard someone say that unforgiveness is like setting yourself on fire and hoping the other person dies of smoke inhalation. Unbeknownst to me, I had been keeping the offenders in a prison I had built in my mind. This allowed me to go to that prison and tell them off, torture them, force them to apologize, or anything else that temporarily helped me cope and feel better. The visits made me feel superior and I would make sure that they would serve a life sentence so that the suffering they received would never end. Looking back, I realize that this plan, subconscious though it was, had a fatal flaw. While I visited the offender in prison, I also remained in prison. Maybe that explains why I was so paralyzed that morning in the coffee shop.

The day my dad and I climbed old Winchester he asked me to forgive him for not being there throughout my childhood. It was a decision I had the power to make, not a feeling I waited to have. Forgiveness was the key that let us both out of our internal prisons.

To this day, every time I take the trash out to the curb for garbage pickup, I am reminded to take out the internal clutter that people dump either on purpose or by accident. Keeping my heart trash-free through constant forgiveness helped to keep my soul clean and gave joy a place to reside.

Along my journey I had to learn that forgiveness is not minimizing the seriousness of the offense. It's not instant restoration of trust or resuming the relationship without changes. Forgiveness is not a warm fuzzy feeling or saying what they did was okay. It's not even denying the hurt that happened. The hurt and the wounds are as real as the garbage in the coffee shop. Bag it up and take it out.

I remember like it was yesterday, the pain in the old man's eyes that pushes me forward as though I am haunted by the thought of ending up as he did. It reminds me that if I use the measuring stick of the past to measure the future, I'll never get farther than my past. I refuse to let my history steal my destiny or taint my legacy. I have noticed that there are those who live a life of regret, live in the past, and talk about what could have been, while those that live a life of significance learn from the past and let it go, so they are free to move from the prison of regret and live their legacy.

2. Journaling - Write it down

I often forget what I should remember and remember things I should forget. So, I choose to write down the things that matter. After all, the shortest pencil is longer than the longest memory. I have made a practice of writing down my goals and taking notes every time I hear wisdom that can help me. I feel like the words on the page make me accountable. They stare at me until I move into action. I often think of the lady at The Tattered Page who helped me purchase the first of many journals. As I have gotten older and observed people, I have found that most people live their life, then look back at it. By writing it down or keeping a journal, I have reversed that - I write it down, then live it!

I constantly draw the target by writing down my goals, values and priorities. I write them and read them like a script of a desired character I want to play. They keep me focused. After all, I can't hit the target if I can't see the target. My writing is the target and the journal is the tool. This is not a new idea. As a matter of fact, it's a very old idea. The concept was recorded in 606 B.C. by an author named Habakkuk when he wrote, "Write the vision, and make it plain upon tables, that he may run that readeth it."

If it worked for him, I decided it would work for me. So, I write it. Then, I can read it. Then, I can run with it. It's like my own personal GPS. My journal has become my life map.

Of all the things that have helped me in personal growth, writing out my values and connecting them to my goals keeps me living with priority while documenting my legacy.

> My journal has become my life map.

It's in the journal that creativity is birthed and expressed. Just like a mechanic needs a wrench or a carpenter needs a hammer, I need a journal. It's my tool of choice and it serves alongside me to clarify my ideas and insights. It helps me affirm the areas where I am making progress.

It's here I record and strategize plans to reach higher levels of life. Every day, its pages bear witness to the things I am grateful for, which in return keeps me positive and energetic.

Taking time to write things down creates much needed space in my life. It forces me to have a place to stop and think. It's when I disconnect, so I can reset and reevaluate.

Like so many people, I can stay as busy as an octopus on roller skates. However, activity does not always equate into productivity. What gets measured, gets accomplished.

3. Integrity - Walk Tall

I have learned to walk tall because I have nothing left to prove and nothing left to hide. Walking tall is the first step to leaping tall obstacles. I think success is measured by what we do, but significance is measured by who we are. I once heard it said that hard days and disappointments in life build character. But I think our true character doesn't even show up until we face hard days and disappointments.

I have often asked myself *who am I when no one is looking*? The answer to the question determines my level of integrity.

I have determined to walk tall, as the old man called it, and to walk tall all the time. I have been working

> Integrity is not something that you say you have, it's something that you show you have.

on a better me since those three days with the old man, and I have discovered that integrity is the cornerstone to building a good character. The legacy that I live will be the legacy that I leave. I get to choose to be honest, to be consistent, to be the same person in private that I am in public. My level of integrity determines my level of influence, trust, respect, and ultimately what I will be remembered for. Integrity is not something that you say you have, it's something that you show you have. I think it was Mark Twain who said, "If you tell the truth, you don't have to remember anything".

4. Identity - Dog Tags

I found my purpose when I discovered my identity. My dad helped me with this the day we climbed old Winchester. We talked from sunset to sunrise and he told me how proud he was of me. That gave me the confidence to step out in courage. I discovered that finding my identity pointed me in the right direction. It pointed me toward the right values and dreams. It helped me to ensure that I didn't have my ladder propped against the wrong building. In other words, I was no longer climbing a ladder to reach a destination that didn't reflect my hopes and dreams. Finding my identity didn't happen overnight. It was a process that took place under the spotlight of self-evaluation, answering questions like:

> What do I value?
> Who is a person that I admire and what qualities do I want to mimic?
> What am I passionate about?
> What will I fight for?

What makes me want to get out of bed in the morning?
What would I be willing to do for free?
What things do I do that gives me the most fulfillment?

I came to realize that I can't set goals that are even worth reaching if they are not connected to a value that I own. The values that I own reflect the person that I am. Yes, I am convinced that my identity is the doorway to my destiny. Finding out who I am helped me determine what I would do, and what is my purpose. Identity also helped me to insure my integrity, because integrity would not allow me to compromise my identity.

5. Attitude - A Glass of Lemonade

I have the most fun with this one! I find myself drinking lemonade often, if for no other reason, just to reminisce about the old man and the lesson he taught me about attitude. Yep, good ole #5! Number 5 has allowed me to enjoy, and sometimes simply laugh out loud, at this wonderful journey we call life. I know that I can't always choose what I go through, but I can choose how I go through it. We keep lemonade in the refrigerator at home all the time, every season, just as a reminder that when life throws lemons at

> With my words I instruct, but it with my attitude I inspire.

me, I catch them and make lemonade. Nowadays, I make my living teaching and encouraging others. In doing so, I have come to observe that some things are better caught than taught. My approach is to instruct and inspire. Therefore, with my words I instruct, but it with my attitude I inspire. Someone long before me coined the phrase *attitude is everything*. I would add, *my attitude affects my outlook on everything*.

I am often reminded of the day my wife and I took our kids to a local carnival and both kids got to pick a helium filled balloon. Our son picked a green balloon that was huge, and our daughter picked a red balloon that was a bit smaller thinking she didn't want it to be too big for her little 5-year-old self. Shortly thereafter, we spied the cotton candy man and they each got some pink cotton candy on a stick. However, her love for cotton candy proved to be greater than her love for her balloon. Fully enjoying the last of her cotton candy and making sure that not a trace could be found on the paper stick, she accidently let go of her red balloon. We had a scene and a very disappointed little girl, who instantly decided that she would rather have a green balloon because her big brother still had his. In her little girl mind she thought green balloons were better because they didn't fly away. I took the opportunity to share with her the same lesson that I get to teach to adult boys and girls. It's not the color or the size that cause a balloon to soar; it's all about what's inside!

6. Friends - Lightning on the Porch

If number five is the most fun, then number six has been the most fulfilling. Friends are a game changer. Friends give me the opportunity to love, to learn about myself, to stretch my ideas and maybe even to test out a good joke. It takes courage and time to build healthy friendships, but the investment is well worth the pay off. My friends have earned the right to step on my toes because they can do it without messing up my shine. They see the worst in me, but believe the best in me. They encourage, inspire, lift up, challenge, and simply help me become a better me!

The old man had a unique way of telling me of the friends I should seek out. I am confident that I am where I am today because of them.

The Hercules - They are the friends that have fought for me and they fight for what I fight for. They bring their own strength and talent to the table. They are strong and secure enough to lift me up to a higher level.

The Hound Dogs - They are the friends that have helped me pursue my dreams. Because they have a common interest, they won't allow me to get off course.

The Huckleberries - They are the friends that have my back no matter what! I have since added to the list. I couldn't let the old man have all the good ideas. I just figured that he gave me a foundation to build on. I have added...

The Sponsor - They are friends that believe in me. They see who I could be, even when I don't see it myself.

The Charger - They are the friends that charge me up. They encourage and build me up when I need refueling. I also have...

The Coach - They are the few friends that stretch my thinking. They are allowed to put a demand on my life. Last but not least is…

The Partner - This is the friend that stands shoulder to shoulder in the trenches, perhaps even face to face. This friend happens to be my best friend and also my amazing wife.

I don't think I am much different than others when I say I need friends because I have needs. I need to be heard and understood. The old man listened to me. I felt as though he understood me, and it helped validate the feelings that I wrestled with so long ago. I am no longer ashamed to admit that I long for encouragement because sometimes life will drain you. I also have a need to be included with no strings attached. I have made it my personal agenda to have these friends in my life, and to be these type of friends to others.

7. Positive Thinking - Pink Elephants

The first thing I had to change was my mind. I was defeated before I ever started because of the lies I had chosen to believe. I now refer to that time as the days of stinking thinking. I am a true believer in the fact that *what I think about, is where I have, and will go about*. Both obstacles and opportunities have served to persuade me that success is determined by the size of my thinking. I have run off the pink elephants by making sure that my thinking is bigger than the elephants. I don't think about how bad things can go. I imagine what it might look like if I take on the task and win. Somehow, the old man convinced me to stop thinking about what might go wrong and use my energy to think through what might go right. I guess you could say that pink elephants don't have an access pass to the fields of possibilities that live in my mind. It seems as though what I think about, is what I talk about, and what I talk about, tells my brain to find a way to make it happen. Maybe there is a positive side to everything, and maybe it just takes positive thinking to find it.

8. Face the Fear - That's Not Your Problem

Life has thrown a lot of challenges and obstacles my way since my conversation with the old man many years ago. I chose not to run or hide. Cowards run, and cowards never climb mountains. My problems have never been my problems. It's how I face the problems that determine my success or failure. Getting rid of the wrong thinking from lesson #7 helps me face the problem. I realize that I can't solve my problems with the same stinking thinking that helped me create the problem. Victories don't always go to the strongest and the fastest. Sooner or later, the person who wins is the man who thinks he can. The more I began to cultivate these nine lessons, the more I realize how they fueled each other. It was like each one added strength to the other ones. They begin to multiply.

For example, the difference between a problem and an opportunity is our thinking and our attitude towards it. My thinking and my attitude determine how I view the problems that arise because every opportunity has a problem and every problem has an opportunity. I learned along the way that it was less stressful to change my perspective than stress out over the problem. Very simply, I decided that if a problem was out of my control, then it was not my problem to own. Therefore, my resolve is to not waste good sleep, energy, or time on a problem that I don't own. On the other hand, if it is within my ability and interest to face the problem, even it is intimidating, I feel the fear and face it anyway. The best way to get rid of fear is by action. The longer I put things off, the louder the voice of fear gets. So, I shut fear down by facing the problem.

> Every opportunity has a problem, and every problem has an opportunity.

9. Goals - Old Winchester

I am now living a dream life, because I dared to dream it, broke it into goal-sized daily tasks and went to work. Whenever procrastination tries to take over a dream, I muster up my best old man impersonation and say, *'The first two letters in goal are 'go'. Now go climb that mountain!'* I have climbed many mountains, and one obstacle after another, simply by acting, checking my goals and my behavior and making sure they match. Anybody that brags about what they are going to do tomorrow probably did the same thing yesterday.

It was a challenge for me to move from just trying to survive, to setting goals, to thrive. Rather than just set arbitrary goals, I began to put them into categories that matter the most to me, so I could keep a balanced approach. I also learned that as my goals evolved, they changed with seasons. My goals would change when my values got shifted or adjusted based on the seasons of life. But the categories have remained consistent.

Goal Categories:

> Adventure
> Character
> Emotional
> Family
> Financial
> Health
> Intellectual
> Legacy
> Professional
> Spiritual

Old Winchester was my first climb and it gave me the faith to face bigger goals and overcome bigger obstacles. I learned that if my goals aren't expandable, then they are expendable.

> If my goals aren't expandable, then they are expendable.

I shared those nine valuable lessons many times with so many people that it helped solidify them in my own life. People's desire to hear the nine lessons of legacy became so great that I eventually started "The Legacy Conference". I've shared with thousands of people in conferences, workshops, and small coaching groups how to apply the nine lessons taught to me by a bitter old man. Those lessons changed my life, and now many countless others.

Twenty-three years have passed. Feelings of rejection, anxiety, abandonment and fear still try to poke their nasty heads up from time to time. But I have learned not to keep company with them, thanks to an old man that I often wished I could introduce to my family. Then again, maybe I don't. He was quite grumpy. I've been back many times, even driven by the old ranch, but there were no signs of life there. He must have passed on shortly after I left. I often wish I could thank him and tell him what I have done with his advice, even how my kids have benefitted from his warnings.

Through the years I have repeated the words and retold the stories to my kids so often that they can talk about them better than I can. They were told as bedtime stories and life lessons as they grew up. My hopes are that they will pass them on to the next generation. After all, that's what living a legacy is all about. It seems every time I blink, another year passes by. I find myself trying harder to live with my eyes wide open and trying to keep the sand from falling so fast.

15

Seasons of Life

As the kids got older, it was a rare occasion that got us all together. But there we were discussing a graduation party that we just had for our daughter. We were discussing her future, schools she might attend, and places she wants to see as I remind her that the world is her stage. At the same time, our son was telling us about this girl that he had been keeping close contact with since meeting her on one of our many trips to see their grandpa. I was trying my best to embrace the present and hold off another season that seemed to be forcing its way into our lives.

We had made it a practice to dream about possible options and dream about what life could look like every time a new season brought us to a crossroad. I reminded myself yet again to face the fear. I started feeling more and more like the old man that I once met, constantly reinforcing the nine nuggets he gave me. My kids had no idea the legacy they would inherit because of an old man they never met.

The discussions about school options and travel left my wife and I feeling that an empty nest was next in our lives, and we were both unsure how to feel about that. It's a very unfamiliar and peculiar place in life, when your kids have become adults and they are launching into new arenas and climbing their own mountains. It's like they have reached the summer time of their lives. Ironically, parents that gave them life are approaching the fall of their lives; leaves me wondering if I can handle the new season of my life. But I have learned to face the fear and keep moving forward. With a full heart, we listened to our kids as they shared their dreams and hopes.

Conversation was slowing, and the night was settling in when the abrupt ring of the phone brought us all back to the reality of today.

"I'll get it," I said. "Hello?"

Another season was starting, and life again was throwing lemons my way. The voice on the other end was a friend of my dad informing me that they had found him on top of old Winchester and he had apparently died of a heart attack. I couldn't believe what I was hearing. He was still young. We were all going out there later this summer. As tears filled my eyes, I realized again the importance of every day. I didn't have any regrets. I was sad and happy at the same time. I blinked repeatedly to process the tears. I informed my family that I would fly out the next day and have them join me after arrangements had been made.

Within 24 hours, plans were made, and I was alone in his house. You would think that I would be sad, but the reality was my heart was full. I fell asleep with vivid memories of the last 23 years. I awoke the next morning knowing that I would have a couple days to myself before the memorial. Feeling a bit worn out from the sudden travel and lack of sleep, I thought I would visit the old coffee shop. Maybe I'd write down some thoughts for the memorial service.

The town really hadn't changed too much from those earlier days of my visit. I had stopped in occasionally in my travels, but it had been years since I had done so. I walked through the door, only to hear the old brass bell still doing its job and announcing the arrival of all who entered. I couldn't help but feel a bit melancholy as I remembered my first time there. How much I had changed.

I ordered my coffee, the barista having no idea how significant this place was to me. I found a table and began to make some notes on my legal pad. That hadn't changed. I still liked to write things out the old-fashioned way. I laughed to myself as I noticed the old leather chairs had been thrown out and replaced with tables, giving people more room to use their computers. The place was busy with the morning rush, like it was those many years ago.

I sat trying to write, but was consumed by the memories that changed the direction of my life. For the first time in a long time, my mind was void of what to say. So, I just sat. From my table I saw old Winchester and retraced my climb with my dad.

Such a defining moment for me, one that I will never forget. I traced out every step, remembered every conversation, and tried to recapture the feelings of that day. I pretended I could see that purple sky and the miracle of friendship that happened between a father and his son. The deeper I was in thought, the more I became totally oblivious to the fact that the shop had emptied out its morning rush and the place had grown very quiet. It was the empty stillness of the room that magnified the sound of that old brass bell as yet another customer entered.

I didn't look up or pay attention until I heard, "I'll take a white chocolate Americano" in a voice that I couldn't have forgotten in 100 years. I was jolted out of memory lane, thinking I was hearing things.

As I looked up to the voice, I couldn't believe my eyes. I thought maybe it just looked like...

The old man! Somehow, he looked happier. Walked a little different too and seemed as though he had more pep in his step. He'd have to be well over 100 by now! It's his eyes, the eyes that seemed so intriguing years ago are once again looking my way with that familiar glare that gave him away. He looked my way, winked, and headed towards me.

"This seat taken?" He asked with a laugh.

I couldn't even find the words to....

"The night you drove away from my house you thanked me," he said. "Well, now it's time for me to thank you, for giving me the life I always wanted. Thanks for taking your own advice.

My own advice! I couldn't process what was happening fast enough. What do you mean?

"The night you drove away from my place, I told you that I was counting on you to take the nine nuggets of advice and give me a chance to redeem my regrets."

"Yeah, I remember that," I managed to say.

"You did it!" he exclaimed. "You lived a life of legacy!"

He pulled out the journal that I had written in many years ago. It was weathered and worn like it had been read and studied many times over.

"Wait! How did you get my journal?" I asked. "That should be home on my bookshelf!" I proclaimed.

"It's my journal," the old man said. "We wrote it many years ago." He smiled like he knew something I didn't.

"Let me explain," he said. "You had the rare opportunity to see how your life could have turned out if you would have let fear take over and never pursued your dreams. That morning at the coffee shop, all those years ago, I introduced you to yourself. You had a conversation with the bitter, alone, and regretful you. Not much of a legacy! But look at us now!" he said.

Tears of joy began to run down my face as I was having my light bulb moment.

"Nobody can make you change. Only you have the power to change," he said, "People can help. They can encourage and coach, but ultimately the power is not in somebody. The power to create a better you, is in you. Always was and always will be."

With that he handed me our journal. "I guess you could say this is our Legacy Journal," he said.

We stood. He thanked me. We embraced. Then, he walked out the door.

I opened the journal for the first time in many years and read the words on the inside cover:

Live Your Legacy

I laughed with a heart full of joy, realizing the contrast of emotions and outlook I had from the very first time I sat in this coffee shop.

"I will," I said out loud. "I will!"

Discussion Questions

Chapter 1

1. What questions have I avoided asking about myself? Have I avoided asking due to fear, insecurities, behavior?

Chapter 2

1. Who is the friend that you can have a conversation with regarding hurts and healing?

Chapter 3

1. Who do you need to forgive?

2. What pain from the past can you leverage into power for today?

Chapter 4

1. What hopes, dream, and values should you write into the chapters of your life?

Chapter 5

1. What thing do you need to forgive yourself for?

2. What words of shame will you eliminate and what words of affirmation do you need to embrace? Start today.

Chapter 6

1. Who are you? What are you good at? What are you passionate about?

2. What does your life movie look like?

Chapter 7

1. What negative circumstance do I need to find the positive in?

2. What is the positive?

Chapter 8

1. What friends are in my inner circle?

2. What qualities in a friend should I be looking for?

Chapter 9

1. What repetitive negative thoughts do I need to eliminate?

2. What 10 things am I grateful for right now?

Chapter 10

1. What problems am I carrying that is out of my control and I need to lay down?

Chapter 11

1. What mountain (Goal) do I want to climb right now? Write down start and finish date.

Chapter 12

1. Who can I thank for investing in my Legacy?

Chapter 13

1. Who is proud of you?

2. Who are you proud of?

3. Have you told them?

Chapter 14

1. What am I experiencing right now that I should relish?

Chapter 15

1. What do I want the 83-year-old me to say about the life I lived?

2. What is my Legacy?

3. If you had the opportunity to sit down with the 83-year-old you, what advice would he/she give you?

WRITE A LEGACY PARAGRAPH

Your life map starts with one paragraph. Write a Legacy paragraph as a declaration to yourself that you choose to live by design rather than default.

Here are some questions to get you started:

1. If I connected with the 83-year-old me, what would I want him or her to say about us?

2. What words do I want to be used when people are talking about my life?

3. How do I want others to feel in my presence?

4. What would I like my loved ones to say about me?

5. What regrets do I want to avoid?

6. What will my life show that I valued?

7. What habits am I building to live the life I desire?

8. What am I doing today that is securing my tomorrow?

9. What goals will I set that reinforce my legacy?

You can use these questions as a guide in writing your Legacy paragraph. The questions are also printed for you in the Legacy Journal that you can purchase at kenhubbard.org

You've read the book. Now experience the movement!

Attend the Living Legacy event live.

Don't wait to leave a legacy.

Begin the practical steps today and start living a legacy.

Find out more information or book your own living legacy event at:

KenHubbard.org

Final thought... I hope "Living Your Legacy" will serve as a constant reminder that...

Where you're at, is not where you have to stay.

Connect with Ken
online at:
kenhubbard.org

or on Facebook at:
facebook.com/kennhubbard

Made in the USA
San Bernardino, CA
09 February 2019